This

Sandra Lee
semi-homemade®

Cool Kids'
Cooking

book belongs to:

....

Meredith® Books Des Moines, Iowa

Copyright© 2006 Sandra Lee Semi-Homemade® All rights reserved. Printed in China.
Library of Congress Control Number 2006923866 ISBN-13: 978-0-696-23265-7 ISBN-10: 0-696-23265-0
Published by Meredith® Books. Des Moines, Iowa.

sem·i·home·made

adj. **1:** a stress-free solution-based formula that provides savvy shortcuts and affordable, timesaving tips for overextended do-it-yourself families. **2:** a quick and easy equation wherein 70% ready-made convenience products are added to 30% fresh ingredients with creative personal style, allowing everyone to take 100% of the credit for something that looks, feels, or tastes homemade **3:** a foolproof resource for having it all—and having the time to enjoy it **4:** a method created by Sandra Lee for home, garden, crafts, beauty, food, fashion, and entertaining wherein everything looks, tastes, and feels as if it was made from scratch.

dedication

To my nieces and nephews:
Austen, Blake, Brandon, Bryce, Danielle, Katie, Scott, Stephanie, and Taner
Who taught me the true meaning of kewl.
Hangin' with you makes me the happiest aunt on the planet.
May all your wishes have wings.

special thanks

To my fun family at the Food Network:
Brooke, Bob, Irene, Susan, Mory, and Santos—
You're awesome!

acknowledgments

To my Dream Team:
Your work is totally out of this world!
Jeff—The Coolest Culinary Cat
Jack—The Main Man
Bob—The First Mate
Doug—The Rock Star
Jim—The Boss Man
Jan—The Head Cheerleader
Matt—The Top Dawg
Mick—The Designer Dude
Michael—The Agent Extraordinaire
Pamela—The Writing Wonder Girl
Jessica—The Cleanup Captain

Contents

Bright Breakfasts 16

Meal Mania 48

Lazy Day Lunches 30

Everyday TV Dinners 64

Letter from Sandy

Move over, Mom and Dad. In the kitchen, kids rule!

Taco Mac … Potato Bombs … Dino Cookies … what do all these bodalicious dishes have in common? You! Cook 'em, eat 'em, and show 'em off. I'll show you how to do it step-by-step the Semi-Homemade® way. It's a cool kind of cooking by the numbers. Start with 70% stuff off the store shelves, add 30% of your own brand of mojo, and give it up for a dish that's 100% yours. Now that's math you can count on.

Hey, this stuff isn't hard! If you can stir, you can cook. I started baking from the Bisquick® box when I was 10 years old. My 6-year-old nephew, Bryce, dials up dinner, all by himself. My 9-year-old niece, Stephanie, bakes up batches of fun, while12-year-old Austen makes mad movie munchies. Come weekends, 13-year-old Danielle serves up super snacks at sleepovers, and when it's time for lunch, 14-year-old Scott is the man with the pan. Even 5-year-old Blake cranks up TV dinners, with a little help from 13-year-old Brandon, who can't get enough of brainiac snacks. And while 3-year-old Katie can't cook (yet!), she sure does like to shake things up in the kitchen.

When you cook, you get to choose, so fix your fave. Get jammin' in the a.m. with a Good Morning Parfait, make Mini Melts for lunch, then flaunt your stuff in front of the fam with Cowboy Meat Loaf for dinner. If you gotta eat your veggies, power-packed Pasta Zoo with Peas and Carrots is the way to go. And homework is much easier to swallow when you have smart snacks like BLT Dip and Pizza Braids. Smooth move whipping up that P.B. Smoothie—it'll go down slooow good with Cheesecake Sandwiches at an after-school jam session. And when you want something wet and wicked, a Tropical Cooler is "chill" the one.

Think you're clueless in the kitchen? It's all good. Straight up instructions come with every recipe. Get the 4-1-1 on lingo and tools, plus radical tips on how to create meals of your own. And every dish is ready in a hot minute, leaving you time for kickin' it with friends.

Learn how, then school the peeps … or show the 'rents wazup. Later on the mall … but for now, the kitchen's where it's cookin'.

Dish delish!

Sandra Lee

Sandra Lee

Points for Parents

Hey, Mom and Dad, here we go!

The kids are in the kitchen tonight and cooking up some boss foods. But here and there, they're going to need some backup—from you. Be there to give them a hand when the going gets rough. Remember, if you don't think your little dudes are ready to handle certain projects (accidents with sharp knives and superhot liquids can make cooking seriously not fun!), you need to step in and take charge. In fact, your best bet for safe cooking fun is to hang tight with your budding new cooks as they get acquainted with the ins and outs of the kitchen. Just because it's easy for you to slice and dice an onion or drain pasta doesn't mean smaller hands and arms can do the same thing right away. It all takes practice and a little bit of help from all-knowing grown-ups like you.

Before each cooking project begins, let the peeps pick out a recipe they want to try, then read over it with them carefully. Talk over what they may need help with and explain why that help is necessary. Let them know it's not because you don't trust them or think they're not capable—it's just that you want them to be safe and have fun. Also be super clear on what recipes they shouldn't be mixing and mashing in the kitchen when you're not around.

As the parent, if you think your children can handle the harder tasks themselves, let them give it a try while you stand by. With a little bit of prompting and encouragement, your kids can be preparing three-course meals for you in no time. And if you're lucky, they'll even clean up afterward!

Without their knowing it, your kids will be learning all about boring things like responsibility, creativity, and self-reliance. As long as you don't tell them, they'll be good to go! Get ready to have some wicked fun with food!

On your mark, get set, COOK!

Sense and Safety

Awesome Adults:
Hey, they're your parents for a reason—they actually know stuff! Before you start slinging food, have an adult read through each recipe with you. If you don't understand something, ask questions. Always ask permission before you start cooking and only cook when an adult is at home.

Electrical Lowdown:
Keep mixers, blenders, and other appliances away from water. If one of them falls in while it's plugged in, DON'T TOUCH IT! Ask an adult for help. Dry your hands before plugging in appliances.

Pull the Plug:
Mixers need to be unplugged before the beaters are put in or taken out. Always turn off mixers and blenders before scraping the sides of the bowl or container with a rubber spatula. Also, DO NOT stick your fingers or anything else in the toaster to remove stuck toast. Ask an adult for assistance.

Hot Stuff:
Dishes pulled from the oven or stove are HOT and will be for a while. Don't put hot dishes directly on the counter—always place them on a hot pad. Wear oven mitts when handling anything hot. Turn saucepan handles toward the inside of the stove so you don't bump into them. Also, open lids on saucepans away from you so the steam doesn't burn your face.

Microwave This!:
Not everything can go in the microwave. Make sure the dishes you use are microwave-safe—if you're not sure, ask an adult. Never put foil or anything metal in the microwave.

Be Sharp:
You know not to run with knives or scissors—that's a no-brainer. But also remember sharp utensils need to be picked up by their handles. Don't dump them into a sinkful of soapy water—you might forget they're in there!

Keep It Clean:
Keep your clothes clean (and Mom happy) by wearing an apron and rolling up your sleeves when you cook. Keep your hair pulled back and wash your hands before you start cooking!

Keep your "mitts" safe by using oven mitts to remove hot dishes from the oven or microwave.

Know Your Icons:
Most recipes have some little icons beside the ingredients list. These will help you plan out how much help you need for each dish.

 The helper icon means an adult helper is needed for certain steps in this recipe, such as cutting food with a sharp knife or pouring hot pasta water into a colander. Most recipes call for a helper, unless no cooking, sharp objects, or heat is used. If you think you're old enough to handle these tasks, talk to your 'rents to see if they agree.

 The scissors icon means sharp objects, such as knives or scissors, are needed to complete this recipe. If only a table knife is required, the icon is not used.

 The oven mitt icon means the recipe requires the use of oven mitts. The recipe method usually tells you when to use oven mitts (such as removing dishes from the oven or microwave) but doesn't indicate every instance that mitts should be used (such as returning a hot dish to the oven). Always be careful around a dish that has been removed from the oven.

 The electricity icon means the recipe requires the use of an electrical appliance such as a microwave, toaster, mixer, or blender. Keep all of these items away from water and DON'T TOUCH THEM if they fall in the water.

The steak icon means the recipe calls for raw eggs, poultry, meat, or fish. After touching raw food items, wash your hands and work surfaces well with warm soapy water.

Recipe Reading

* Before you start, read through the entire recipe and make sure you understand what needs to be done.

* Check the list of icons at the side of each recipe (see icon information, page 9) and alert an adult if you need help to complete the recipe.

* Go through the list next to each recipe called "Tools You'll Need." Pull out each tool the recipe calls for and stack it up neatly near your work area.

* Read through your ingredient list and get all the ingredients gathered together in one area.

* Check the refrigerator and pantry to see if you have all the foods you need. If not, make a trip to the grocery store.

* Check the banner above each recipe to see how long it will take to prepare. Make sure you have enough time to complete the recipe.

* Now you can start with step 1 of your chosen recipe. Use good safety habits (see page 9) and clean up as you cook. (This will keep you from having one monster mess at the end!)

When you're done with the recipe, put away all the ingredients and tools, wash all the dirty dishes, and wipe counters clean.

(Illustration of recipe page)

BTC Quiche

Prep 15 minutes Bake 45 minutes Cool 15 minutes Makes 8 servings

Tools you'll need:
* Measuring cups
* Measuring spoons
* Baking sheet
* Aluminum foil
* Medium bowls
* Whisk
* Strainer
* Spoon
* Oven mitts
* Wire cooling rack
* Sharp knife
* Pie server
* Dinner plates

Food you'll need:
1½ cups milk
½ cup shredded cheddar cheese, Kraft
2 large eggs
½ teaspoon salt
⅛ teaspoon ground black pepper
1 can (14.5-ounce) diced tomatoes, Hunt's
1 frozen deep-dish pie shell, thawed
½ cup bacon pieces, Hormel

Here's what you do:

Preheat oven to 375 degrees F. Cover a baking sheet with aluminum foil.

In a medium bowl, using a whisk, beat milk, eggs, cheese, salt, and pepper until combined. Set aside. Using a strainer set over another medium bowl, drain tomatoes; set aside. Discard liquid.

Using a spoon, fill thawed pie shell with drained tomatoes and bacon. Pour egg mixture into pie shell. Place pie shell on prepared baking sheet.

Place baking sheet in preheated oven on the middle rack. Bake for 45 to 50 minutes. (Have an adult insert a table knife near the center of the quiche. If it comes out clean, the quiche is done.) Using oven mitts, remove quiche from oven. Place on wire rack; cool for 15 minutes. Have an adult cut quiche into wedges with a sharp knife. Place on dinner plates with a pie server. Serve warm.

22 Bright Breakfasts

Learn the Lingo

Bake: to cook food in the oven.

Beat: to add air to a mixture by stirring it rapidly with a fork or handheld mixer.

Boil: to cook liquid over high heat on the stovetop. Big bubbles will come to the surface rapidly and break when a liquid is boiling.

Chill: to place a food in the refrigerator to make it cold.

Chop: to use a sharp knife (ask an adult to do this) to cut food, such as onions, into small pieces.

Combine: to mix ingredients together. Most often this is done in a bowl.

Cool: to let a food stand at room temperature until it is no longer hot after it has been cooked.

Drain: to separate a food from liquid by pouring it into a strainer or colander (see illustrations, right). For example, after pasta is cooked in hot water, it is separated from the water before you eat it.

Grease: to spread a layer of fat on a baking sheet to prevent sticking during cooking. Put a sandwich baggie on your hand to keep it from getting dirty, then use it to spread a little butter on the pan.

Measure: to get an exact amount of an ingredient by putting it in a measuring cup or spoon. To

measure liquid ingredients, use a liquid measuring cup (they often have a spout on the top edge; see illustration, right). To measure dry ingredients, use dry measuring cups (see illustration, page 11) that come in sets of different sizes.

Melt: to turn a solid, such as butter, into a liquid by heating it.

Shred: to tear an ingredient, such as lettuce, with your hands or cut it with a knife into small, thin pieces.

Slice: to use a knife to cut a food, such as a peeled banana, into pieces that are the same thickness.

Kitchen Gadgets

Before you start dishing up the grub in the kitchen, take a look at this gadgets chart. These are the top tools you'll need to make awesome food.

Skillet

Liquid Measuring Cup

Heat-Resistant Spatula

Wooden Spoon

Tongs

Dry Measuring Cups

Measuring Spoons

Whisk

Saucepans

Handheld Electric Mixer

Cookie Sheet

Slotted Spoon

Kitchen Shears

Colander

Strainer

Table Knife

Vegetable Peeler

Icing Spatula

Sharp Knife

Juicer

Cutting Board

Wire Cooling Rack

Smart Foodie Checklist

Wipe out bacteria! Raw poultry, eggs, fish, and meat contain bacteria that are harmful until after the food is cooked thoroughly. When cutting up or handling these raw foods, always wash your hands, cutting boards, surfaces, and other utensils well with warm soapy water immediately after handling the raw product. This is very important!

Separate cooked from raw. Place cooked meat, poultry, eggs, or fish in a clean dish. Never place it in the same container or on the same cutting board that you used when the product was raw.

Use a thermometer. To make sure meat, poultry, and fish are cooked thoroughly, have an adult stick an instant-read thermometer into the center of the food. Many recipes specify the temperature the food needs to reach before it is safe (remember, chicken breasts should typically be cooked to 165 degrees F or 170 degrees F) and reheat any leftovers to 165 degrees F.

Say no to raw eggs! Remember, cookie dough often contains raw eggs, and even though it tastes great, it can make you very sick. Play it safe by only eating baked cookies.

Keep cold foods cold. Put all your cold foods and leftovers in the refrigerator as soon as possible. Letting them sit out on the counter encourages bacteria growth, and you certainly don't want to eat that! Never thaw frozen meat by letting it sit out at room temperature. Smaller pieces of meat can be thawed in the microwave (use the defrost setting and follow the manufacturer's directions) only if you plan on using them right away.

Fresh is best! Use only fresh foods and throw out anything that is spoiled or past its expiration date. Always wash fresh fruits and vegetables thoroughly in cool water.

Wash your hands!

The Cool Cleanup Crew

Suds up in the kitchen! Yucky bacteria can hang out almost anywhere, so keep everything that touches your food as clean as possible. Before you begin cooking, wash your hands for at least 20 seconds with lots of water and soap. When doing dishes, fill a sink with warm soapy water. Scrub pans and utensils until all visible food has been removed, then rinse everything well. Clean all work surfaces with warm soapy water. Keep bacteria at bay by using disposable paper towels to clean anything that has touched raw meat, poultry, or fish. Otherwise the bacteria might make a permanent home in your sponges and dishcloths!

Healthy is Happenin'

Ever heard of the food pyramid? It has tons of useful information, including what food groups are important to keep your body strong. Here's the lowdown on what you need to know about these super rad food groups:

Breads, Rice, Cereal, and Pasta: You need 6 to 9 servings a day (one serving equals 1 slice of bread or ½ cup cooked rice). But the important thing to remember here is that whole grains are better for you, so choose brown rice over white rice and whole grain pasta over white pasta. Your body will be so pumped!

Fruits: You need 2 to 3 servings a day (one serving equals 1 apple or 1 orange). Fruit snacks and fruit-flavor candy don't count—but raisins do!

Vegetables: You need 3 to 4 servings a day (one serving equals ½ cup cooked veggies, like steamed cauliflower, or 1 cup raw veggies, like broccoli). These are packed with vitamins that will turn you from a cool kid into a cool adult (over time, of course!).

Milk, Yogurt, and Cheese: Try to get 2 to 3 servings of dairy a day. Drink 1 cup of milk (which is one serving) with breakfast and you're halfway there!

Meat, Poultry, Dry Beans, and Eggs: Try to get 2 to 3 servings of protein every day (one serving is 1 egg or 3 ounces of meat). Two tablespoons of peanut butter can count as one of your protein servings.

Fats, Oils, and Sweets: This is the category every kid loves but needs to eat less of! These foods have lots of calories and not many healthy nutrients, so be good and keep your candy and chip intake down.

Exercise: Put down that video game and get your body moving! Just about everything counts as exercise (except sitting around watching 'toons), so shoot some hoops, ride your bike, or just dance around the yard. Movement makes your lungs and heart strong, so try to get in at least 30 minutes a day.

Bright Breakfasts

My niece Katie likes her breakfasts bright and early. At 3 years old, she's into everything, which helps if your job is a toddling taste tester. When her brothers Blake and Brandon whip up new recipes, Katie gives them a finicky fork up … or down. If she likes it, it's a keeper. If not, it's floor food. When mornings are warp speed, Grammy's Granola keeps it caz. Gotta love Saturdays—time to take in the 'toons while scarfing down Scrambled Egg Burritos. Sundays, hmmm, how about a BTC Quiche? Eggscellent idea—especially when it's all cooked up quicker than you can say, "Rise and dine."

The Recipes

Egg Nests

Tools you'll need:

* Measuring cups
* Muffin pan with six 2½-inch cups
* Medium bowl
* Spoon
* Small bowl
* Fork
* Sharp knife
* Cutting board
* Oven mitts
* Small bowl
* Aluminum foil
* Table knife
* Dinner plates

Food you'll need:

Butter-flavor cooking spray, *Mazola® Pure*

2½ cups frozen country-style hash brown potatoes, *Ore-Ida®*

¼ cup all-purpose flour

8 large eggs

6 precooked sausage links, *Jimmy Dean®*

Salt and ground black pepper

Here's what you do:

1. Preheat oven to 425 degrees F. Spray the six cups of the muffin pan with cooking spray; set aside.

2. In a medium bowl, using a spoon, toss together hash brown potatoes and flour to coat. In a small bowl, using a fork, beat 2 eggs lightly. Pour over potatoes; stir until well combined.

3. Measure ½ cup of the potato mixture into each muffin cup. With clean hands, press potatoes into bottom and up sides of each cup. Wash hands well.

4. Place muffin pan in preheated oven. Bake for 20 to 25 minutes or until the nests start to brown. While nests bake, have an adult chop sausage links with a sharp knife.

5. Using oven mitts, remove muffin pan from oven. Add some of the chopped sausage to each muffin cup. Carefully crack an egg into a small bowl; slide into one of the nests over sausage. Season lightly with salt and pepper. Repeat with remaining eggs and nests. Cover muffin pan with aluminum foil.

6. Return muffin pan to oven. Bake for 15 to 18 minutes or until egg is desired doneness. Using oven mitts, remove muffin pan from oven.

7. Have an adult help you carefully remove each nest from muffin cup by running a table knife along the edge and lifting it out. Place each nest on a dinner plate. Serve hot.

Scrambled Egg Burritos

Start to Finish 20 minutes Makes 4 servings

Here's what you do:

1 In a large bowl, using a whisk, beat together eggs, cheese, and bacon; set aside.

2 Place butter in a large nonstick skillet. Place on burner; turn burner to medium. Heat until butter is melted. Add egg mixture to skillet. Using a heat-resistant spatula, flip one part of the egg mixture at a time until all the eggs are cooked. Remove skillet from heat.

3 Stack tortillas on a microwave-safe plate. Cover stack with a paper towel. Microwave on high setting (100% power) for 20 seconds or until warm. Using oven mitts, remove from the microwave.

4 To make each burrito, place a tortilla on a flat surface. Place $\frac{1}{2}$ cup of the egg mixture on the tortilla. Wrap tortilla around the eggs to form a burrito.

5 Serve 2 burritos topped with $\frac{1}{4}$ cup picante sauce on each of 4 dinner plates. Serve warm.

Note: These burritos can be made ahead of time by preparing through step 4 and refrigerating. When ready to eat, reheat burritos in the microwave on high setting (100% power) for 3 minutes.

Tools you'll need:

* Measuring cups
* Large bowl
* Whisk
* Large nonstick skillet
* Heat-resistant spatula
* Microwave-safe plate
* Paper towels
* Oven mitts
* 4 dinner plates

Food you'll need:

8	large eggs
1	cup shredded Mexican cheese blend, *Kraft*®
$\frac{1}{2}$	cup real bacon pieces, *Hormel*®
2	tablespoons butter
8	taco-size (8-inch) flour tortillas, *Mission*®
1	cup medium picante sauce, *Pace*® *Organic*

Mini Breakfast Pizzas

Prep 10 minutes Bake 10 minutes Makes 8 pizzas

Tools you'll need

* Measuring cups
* Measuring spoons
* Baking sheet
* Aluminum foil
* Sharp knife
* Cutting board
* Toaster
* Medium bowl
* Whisk
* Large nonstick skillet
* Heat-resistant spatula
* Oven mitts
* Wire cooling rack
* Dinner plates

Food you'll need:

2	tomatoes
4	English muffins, split, *Thomas'*®
8	large eggs
1/4	cup milk
1/2	teaspoon bottled chopped garlic, *Christopher Ranch*®
1/2	teaspoon salt
1/4	teaspoon ground black pepper
2	tablespoons butter
1	package (6-ounce) Canadian bacon slices, *Hormel*®
2	cups shredded mozzarella cheese, *Kraft*®

Here's what you do:

1 Preheat oven to 350 degrees F. Line a baking sheet with aluminum foil; set aside. Have an adult slice tomatoes with a sharp knife.

2 Working in batches, toast the English muffin halves in a toaster; carefully remove English muffins from toaster. In a medium bowl, using a whisk, combine eggs, milk, garlic, salt, and pepper; set aside.

3 Place butter in a large nonstick skillet. Place on burner; turn burner to medium. Heat until butter is melted. Add egg mixture to skillet. Using a heat-resistant spatula, flip one part of the egg mixture at a time until all the eggs are cooked. Remove from heat.

4 To make pizzas, arrange English muffin halves on prepared baking sheet. Top each English muffin half with 1 to 2 tomato slices, a slice of Canadian bacon, and 1/3 cup of the egg mixture. Sprinkle each with 1/4 cup cheese.

5 Place baking sheet in oven. Bake for 10 minutes or until cheese is melted and bubbly. Using oven mitts, remove from oven. Place baking sheet on wire rack; cool for a few minutes. Using the spatula, transfer mini pizzas to dinner plates.

BTC Quiche

Prep 15 minutes **Bake** 45 minutes **Cool** 15 minutes **Makes** 8 servings

Tools you'll need:

* Measuring cups
* Measuring spoons
* Baking sheet
* Aluminum foil
* 2 medium bowls
* Whisk
* Strainer
* Spoon
* Oven mitts
* Wire cooling rack
* Sharp knife
* Pie server
* Dinner plates

Food you'll need:

1½ cups milk

1 cup shredded cheddar cheese, *Kraft*®

3 large eggs

½ teaspoon salt

¼ teaspoon ground black pepper

1 can (14.5-ounce) diced tomatoes, *Hunt's*®

1 frozen deep-dish pie shell, thawed

⅓ cup real bacon pieces, *Hormel*®

Here's what you do:

1 Preheat oven to 375 degrees F. Cover a baking sheet with aluminum foil.

2 In medium bowl, using a whisk, beat milk, cheese, eggs, salt, and pepper until combined. Set aside. Using a strainer set over another medium bowl, drain tomatoes; set aside. Discard liquid.

3 Using a spoon, fill thawed pie shell with drained tomatoes and bacon. Pour egg mixture into pie shell. Place pie shell on prepared baking sheet.

4 Place baking sheet in preheated oven on the middle rack. Bake for 45 to 50 minutes. (Have an adult insert a table knife near the center of the quiche. If it comes out clean, the quiche is done.) Using oven mitts, remove quiche from oven. Place on wire rack; cool for 15 minutes. Have an adult cut quiche into wedges with a sharp knife. Place on dinner plates with a pie server. Serve warm.

Apple Spice Pancake Roll-Ups

Start to Finish 15 minutes Makes 8 servings

Here's what you do:

1. In medium bowl, using a wooden spoon, stir together pancake mix, apple juice, and pumpkin pie spice until well mixed; set aside.

2. Spray a large skillet with cooking spray. Place on burner; turn burner to medium. Heat until a drop of water sizzles. Drop $\frac{1}{3}$ cup batter into skillet for each pancake. Cook about 3 pancakes at a time.

3. Cook pancakes on one side for 3 to 4 minutes or until the bubbles that form begin to pop. Using a heat-resistant spatula, flip each pancake. Cook for another 2 to 3 minutes. (Both sides should be golden brown.) Remove skillet from heat. Using the spatula, transfer pancakes to plates. Repeat until all batter is used.

4. With a table knife, spread 1 tablespoon apple butter on each pancake. Place one sausage link at the edge of each pancake. Roll pancakes around links. Place toothpicks through roll-ups to hold them together.

5. Place roll-ups on a microwave-safe plate. Microwave, uncovered, on high setting (100% power) for 2 to 3 minutes or until warm. Using oven mitts, remove from microwave. Transfer to dinner plates.

Tools you'll need:

* Measuring cups
* Measuring spoons
* Medium bowl
* Wooden spoon
* Large skillet
* Heat-resistant spatula
* Plates
* Table knife
* Wooden toothpicks
* Microwave-safe plate
* Oven mitts
* Dinner plates

Food you'll need:

2 cups just-add-water pancake mix, *Aunt Jemima® Complete*

1½ cups apple juice, *Hansen's®*

2 teaspoons pumpkin pie spice, *McCormick®*

Canola oil cooking spray, *Mazola® Pure*

1 cup apple butter, *Smucker's®*

1 package (7-ounce) precooked turkey breakfast sausage links, *Butterball®*

Fruity French Toast

Prep 15 minutes **Chill** 1 hour **Bake** 1 hour **Stand** 10 minutes **Makes** 12 servings

Tools you'll need:

* Measuring cups
* Measuring spoons
* 13×9-inch baking dish
* Table knife
* Spoon
* Medium bowl
* Whisk
* Plastic wrap
* Oven mitts
* Wire cooling rack
* Heat-resistant spatula
* Dinner plates

Food you'll need:

Butter-flavor cooking spray, *Mazola® Pure*

1   package (20-ounce) frozen French toast sticks, *Krusteaz®*

1   package (8-ounce) cream cheese, *Philadelphia®*

⅓   cup strawberry preserves, *Smucker's®*

3   cups milk

4   large eggs

1   cup pure maple syrup, *Maple Grove Farms®*

1   teaspoon ground cinnamon, *McCormick®*

Here's what you do:

1. Spray a 13×9-inch baking dish with cooking spray. Using a table knife, cut French toast sticks into 1-inch pieces. Arrange evenly in baking dish.

2. Using a table knife, cut cream cheese into ½-inch cubes; sprinkle over French toast sticks. Using a spoon, drop small amounts of strawberry preserves over French toast and cream cheese.

3. In a medium bowl, using a whisk, combine milk, eggs, maple syrup, and cinnamon. Pour over French toast. Loosely cover baking dish with plastic wrap. Place in refrigerator; chill for 1 hour, occasionally pushing French toast down into mixture.

4. Preheat oven to 350 degrees F. Remove plastic wrap from baking dish. Place baking dish in preheated oven on the middle rack. Bake for 1 hour or until golden brown.

5. Using oven mitts, remove baking dish from oven. Place on wire rack; cool for 10 to 15 minutes. Using a heat-resistant spatula, transfer to dinner plates. Serve warm.

Nutty Banana Cakes

Start to Finish 15 minutes Makes 14 cakes

Tools you'll need:

* Measuring cups
* Measuring spoons
* Sharp knife
* Cutting board
* Table knife
* 2 medium bowls
* Fork
* Whisk
* Large skillet
* Heat-resistant spatula
* Dinner plates

Food you'll need:

$\frac{1}{2}$ cup walnuts

2   bananas, peeled

2   cups baking mix, *Bisquick*®

1   cup milk

2   large eggs

1   teaspoon ground cinnamon, *McCormick*®

   Butter-flavor cooking spray, *Mazola® Pure*

Here's what you do:

1 Have an adult finely chop walnuts with a sharp knife; set aside. With a table knife, slice peeled bananas. Place pieces in a medium bowl; mash with a fork, set aside.

2 In another medium bowl, using a whisk, combine baking mix, milk, and eggs until well mixed. Stir in bananas, chopped walnuts, and cinnamon. (Mixture will be a little lumpy.)

3 Spray a large skillet with cooking spray. Place skillet on burner; turn burner to medium. Heat skillet about 1 minute or until a drop of water sizzles across the surface. Pour $\frac{1}{3}$ cup batter into skillet for each pancake. Cook about 3 pancakes at a time.

4 Cook pancakes on one side for 3 to 4 minutes or until bubbles that form begin to pop. Using a heat-resistant spatula, flip each pancake over. Cook for another 2 to 3 minutes. Both sides should be golden brown. Using the spatula, transfer pancakes to dinner plates. Repeat until all the batter is used.

Note: Pancakes can be made ahead of time through step 4 and refrigerated. When ready to serve, reheat in a microwave on high setting (100% power) for 2 to 3 minutes.

Waffle Wheels

Start to Finish 10 minutes Makes 4 sandwiches

Here's what you do:

Using a table knife, cut each banana into 10 slices of equal size (for a total of 20 slices); set aside. Toast waffles in toaster. Carefully remove waffles from toaster.

Using a table knife, spread 2 tablespoons peanut butter on 1 waffle. Top peanut butter with 5 banana slices and 1 tablespoon raisins. Place second waffle on top and sandwich together. Repeat to make a total of 4 sandwiches. Serve on dinner plates.

Tools you'll need:

* Measuring cups
* Measuring spoons
* Table knife
* Toaster
* 4 dinner plates

Food you'll need:

2   bananas, peeled

8   frozen waffles, *Eggo®*

8   tablespoons crunchy peanut butter, *Laura Scudder's®*

¼   cup raisins, *Sun-Maid®*

Good Morning Parfait

Start to Finish 5 minutes Makes 4 servings

Tools you'll need:

* Measuring cups
* 4 sundae glasses
* Spoon

Food you'll need:

4   containers (6 ounces each) French vanilla yogurt, *Yoplait® Original*

2   cups frozen mixed fruit, thawed, *Dole®*

2   cups oats-and-honey granola, *Quaker®*

Here's what you do:

1 Set out 4 sundae glasses. Using a spoon, divide 1 container of yogurt among the glasses. Top yogurt in each glass with some of the thawed frozen fruit. Add some of the granola. Continue parfait layers with the remaining ingredients as desired. Serve immediately.

Grammy's Granola

Prep 10 minutes **Bake** 1 hour **Stand** 1 hour **Makes** 11 cups

Here's what you do:

Preheat oven to 300 degrees F. In a large bowl, using a wooden spoon, stir together old-fashioned oats, instant oatmeal, rice cereal, raisin bran cereal, sunflower seeds, almonds, and raisins. Drizzle with canola oil; mix until thoroughly coated. Drizzle with honey; mix until thoroughly coated. Spread mixture evenly on an ungreased baking sheet.

Place baking sheet in preheated oven. Bake for 1 hour. Stir granola every 15 minutes to ensure even baking. Using oven mitts, remove from oven. Place on a wire rack; let stand for 1 hour or until completely cooled. Transfer granola to large zip-top plastic bags.

Tools you'll need:

* Measuring cups
* Large bowl
* Wooden spoon
* Baking sheet
* Oven mitts
* Wire cooling rack
* 2 large zip-top plastic bags

Food you'll need:

5 cups old-fashioned oats, *Quaker®*

4 packages (1.5 ounces each) cinnamon roll-flavor instant oatmeal, *Quaker®*

1 cup crisp rice cereal, *Kellogg's® Rice Krispies®*

1 cup raisin bran cereal, *Post®*

1 cup sunflower seeds, *David®*

1 cup slivered almonds, *Planters®*

1 cup orange-flavor raisins, *Ocean Spray®*

$2/3$ cup canola oil, *Wesson®*

1 cup honey, *SueBee®*

Lazy Day Lunches

Football … track … clowning around … whether he's on the field, on the phone, or online, my 14-year-old nephew, Scott, is always in motion. This chapter is filled with fun-on-the-run food that active kids like Scott can hip to in a hurry. Whether he's hangin' at the lake—or chillin' in the kitchen—Scott opts for easy eats like Cheese Steak Bagel Bites, Spaghetti Calzones, and Buffalo Pizza, all guaranteed to be a ginormous hit with the It Crowd. Crazy colors, super shapes, and fab flavas—they're all good, and they're all here. No joke! Text the peeps—lunch is at your house today.

The Recipes

Buffalo Pizza

Start to Finish 35 minutes Makes 6 servings

Tools you'll need:

* Measuring cups
* Measuring spoons
* Baking sheet
* Sharp knife
* Cutting board
* Small bowl
* Rubber spatula
* Oven mitts
* Wire cooling rack
* Pizza cutter

Food you'll need:

Canola oil cooking spray, *Mazola® Pure*

1   can (13.8-ounce) refrigerated pizza crust dough, *Pillsbury®*

3   frozen buffalo-style chicken strips, thawed, *Foster Farms®*

1   cup marinara sauce, *Prego®*

2   tablespoons hot wings sauce, *Frank's®*

2   cups shredded Monterey Jack cheese, *Kraft®*

Ranch salad dressing, *Hidden Valley®*

Here's what you do:

Preheat oven to 400 degrees F. Spray baking sheet with cooking spray. With clean hands, unroll pizza dough and place on baking sheet. Spread dough to edges of sheet or to desired thickness. If holes appear in dough, pinch them together. Place baking sheet in preheated oven. Bake for 10 minutes.

Meanwhile, have an adult cut chicken strips into bite-size pieces with a sharp knife; set aside. In a small bowl, using a rubber spatula, stir together marinara sauce and hot wings sauce.

Using oven mitts, remove baking sheet from oven. Place on wire rack. Using the spatula, spread marinara sauce mixture over pizza crust, leaving a 1-inch border around the edge of dough. Sprinkle cheese evenly over sauce and top with chicken.

Using oven mitts, return pizza to oven. Bake for 8 to 10 minutes more or until crust is golden brown and cheese is melted and bubbling.

Using oven mitts, remove pizza from oven. Place on a wire rack. Drizzle with desired amount of ranch salad dressing. Cool for a few minutes. Have an adult use a pizza cutter to cut into slices. Serve warm.

Spaghetti Calzones

Prep 20 minutes   Bake 18 minutes   Cool 5 minutes   Makes 4 calzones

Here's what you do:

Preheat oven to 400 degrees F. Lightly spray baking sheet with cooking spray. Set aside. In small bowl, using a fork, beat together egg and milk; set aside.

Sprinkle a little flour on a flat surface. Sprinkle some of the flour onto a rolling pin. Unroll pizza crust; roll out to a 15×15-inch square. Using a table knife, cut into quarters, making 4 squares of equal size.

Spoon $\frac{1}{2}$ can of spaghetti and meatballs (or $\frac{1}{4}$ cup leftover spaghetti and meatballs) and 1 tablespoon cheese onto half of each dough square. Using a pastry brush, brush edges of square with egg mixture. Fold dough over to form a pocket. Pinch edges together to seal.

Evenly space calzones on prepared baking sheet. Using a pastry brush, brush tops of calzones with egg mixture. Place baking sheet in preheated oven. Bake for 18 to 20 minutes. Using oven mitts, remove baking sheet from oven. Transfer calzones to a wire rack; cool for 5 minutes.

Tools you'll need:

* Measuring cups
* Measuring spoons
* Baking sheet
* Small bowl
* Fork
* Rolling pin
* Table knife
* Spoon
* Pastry brush
* Oven mitts
* Wire cooling rack

Food you'll need:

Canola oil cooking spray, *Mazola® Pure*

1 large egg

1 tablespoon milk

All-purpose flour

1 can (13.8-ounce) refrigerated pizza crust dough, *Pillsbury®*

2 cans (7.5 ounces each) spaghetti and meatballs, *Hormel®*, or 1 cup leftover homemade spaghetti and meatballs

$\frac{1}{4}$ cup shredded mozzarella cheese, *Kraft®*

Sloppy Sandwiches

Prep 30 minutes Bake 13 minutes Makes 8 sandwiches

Tools you'll need:

* Measuring spoons
* Measuring cups
* Baking sheet
* Aluminum foil
* Medium saucepan
* Wooden spoon
* Small bowl
* Fork
* Rolling pin
* Spoon
* Pastry brush
* Oven mitts
* Heat-resistant spatula
* Wire cooling rack

Food you'll need:

8 ounces ground beef

1 packet (1.31-ounce) sloppy joes seasoning mix, *McCormick®*

1 can (6-ounce) tomato paste, *Hunt's®*

1 large egg

1 tablespoon water

All-purpose flour

1 can (16.3-ounce) refrigerated biscuits, *Pillsbury®*

½ cup shredded mozzarella cheese, *Kraft®*

Here's what you do:

1. Preheat oven to 350 degrees F. Line a baking sheet with aluminum foil; set aside.

2. In a medium saucepan, using a wooden spoon, stir together ground beef and sloppy joes seasoning mix. Place saucepan on burner; turn burner to medium-high. Cook and stir about 10 minutes or until meat is browned. Stir in tomato paste until well combined. Remove saucepan from heat.

3. In a small bowl, using a fork, beat together egg and water; set aside.

4. Lightly sprinkle flour on a flat surface and onto a rolling pin. Roll out each biscuit to make a 4-inch circle, turning the biscuit with each roll so it doesn't stick. (If dough starts to stick, use more flour.)

5. For sandwiches, spoon 2 tablespoons meat mixture and 1 tablespoon cheese on one side of each biscuit circle. Using a pastry brush, brush a thin layer of the egg mixture around the edge of each dough circle. Fold dough over meat mixture to form a half-circle. Pinch edges together to seal.* Place on prepared baking sheet. Lightly brush the top of each sandwich with more of the egg mixture.

6. Place baking sheet in preheated oven. Bake for 13 to 15 minutes. Using oven mitts, remove baking sheet from oven. Using a heat-resistant spatula, transfer sandwiches to a wire rack. Cool slightly; serve warm.

*Tip: To make pleats in the crust like in the photo, have an adult use clean kitchen shears or scissors to cut small slits around the edges of the unbaked crust after sealing.

Cordon Bleu Crescents

Prep 20 minutes Bake 18 minutes Cool 2 minutes Makes 8 crescents

Food you'll need:

- 1 can (8-ounce) refrigerated crescent rolls, *Pillsbury®*
- 5 tablespoons condensed cheddar cheese soup, *Campbell's®*
- 8 slices Swiss cheese, *Kraft®*
- 16 thin slices honey ham, *Hillshire Farm®*

Here's what you do:

1. Preheat oven to 375 degrees F. Line a baking sheet with aluminum foil; set aside. Unroll crescent rolls. Separate into triangles. Using a table knife, spread 2 teaspoons cheddar cheese soup in the center of each triangle. Top each triangle with 1 slice Swiss cheese and 2 slices ham.

2. Roll up by starting with the wide end of the triangle and rolling toward the point. Place on baking sheet, point sides down, spacing evenly. Bake in the preheated oven for 18 to 20 minutes or until golden brown. Using oven mitts, remove from oven; place on a wire rack. Cool for 2 to 4 minutes. Using a heat-resistant spatula, transfer crescents to plates.

Cheese Steak Bagel Bites

Prep 20 minutes Bake 10 minutes Makes 8 bagels

Food you'll need:

- 8 mini bagels, presliced, *Thomas'®*
- 16 thin slices roast beef, *Hillshire Farm®*
- 1 can (10.75-ounce) condensed cream of mushroom soup, *Campbell's®*
- 8 slices Monterey Jack cheese, *Kraft®*

Here's what you do:

1. Preheat oven to 350 degrees F. Line a baking sheet with aluminum foil. Arrange the bottom halves of mini bagels on baking sheet. Top each with 2 slices roast beef, 1 tablespoon cream of mushroom soup, and 1 slice cheese. Place the top halves of bagels on top to make sandwiches.

2. Place baking sheet in preheated oven. Bake for 10 to 12 minutes until cheese is melted and sandwiches are heated. Using oven mitts, remove from oven. Using a heat-resistant spatula, transfer bagel bites to dinner plates.*

*Note: If you like, in a small saucepan, combine remaining soup and ¾ cup milk over medium heat until warm. Serve with bagel bites.

Monte Cristo Mania

Prep 20 minutes **Bake** 5 minutes **Cool** 2 minutes **Makes** 4 sandwiches

Here's what you do:

Preheat oven to 375 degrees F. Line a baking sheet with aluminum foil; set aside.

In a large shallow bowl, using a fork, beat together eggs and milk; set aside.

Using a table knife, spread 1 tablespoon of preserves on one side of each bread slice. Layer turkey, ham, and cheese on the jelly side of 4 bread slices. Top with remaining bread slices, jelly sides down.

Place butter in a large skillet. Place on burner; turn burner to medium-high. Heat until butter is melted.

Soak 1 sandwich in egg mixture, about 15 seconds on each side. Transfer sandwich to skillet. Cook for 3 to 4 minutes or until bottom is brown. Using a heat-resistant spatula, carefully turn sandwich. Cook for 3 to 4 minutes more. Transfer cooked sandwich to baking sheet. Repeat with remaining sandwiches.

Place baking sheet in preheated oven. Bake for 5 to 8 minutes or until cheese is melted. Using oven mitts, remove baking sheet from oven. Place on a wire rack; cool for 2 minutes.

Using the spatula, transfer 1 sandwich to each of 4 dinner plates. Using a sifter, sprinkle some powdered sugar over each sandwich. Have an adult slice each sandwich in half with a sharp knife.

Tools you'll need:

* Measuring cups
* Measuring spoons
* Baking sheet
* Aluminum foil
* Large shallow bowl
* Fork
* Table knife
* Large skillet
* Heat-resistant spatula
* Oven mitts
* Wire cooling rack
* 4 dinner plates
* Sifter
* Sharp knife

Food you'll need:

3   large eggs

6   tablespoons milk

1/2 cup raspberry preserves, *Smucker's*®

8   slices white sandwich bread, *Sara Lee*®

4   ounces thinly sliced turkey, *Hillshire Farm*®

4   ounces thinly sliced ham, *Hillshire Farm*®

4   slices Swiss cheese, *Kraft*®

3   tablespoons butter
     Powdered sugar, *C&H*®

Ranch Wraps

Start to Finish 15 minutes Makes 4 wraps

Tools you'll need:

* Measuring cups
* Sharp knife
* Cutting board
* Small bowl
* Spoon
* Paper towels
* Microwave-safe plate
* Oven mitts
* Table knife
* Measuring spoons

Food you'll need:

Torn romaine lettuce, *Ready Pac®*

1   tomato

¼   cup ranch salad dressing, *Hidden Valley®*

¼   cup honey mustard, *French's®*

8   slices ready-to-serve bacon, *Oscar Mayer®*

4   taco-size (8-inch) flour tortillas, *Mission®*

1   package (6-ounce) refrigerated Southwestern-style chicken breast strips, *Hillshire Farm®*

Here's what you do:

With clean hands, shred romaine lettuce and measure 2 cups; set aside. Have an adult use a sharp knife to slice tomato into ¼-inch-thick slices; set aside. In a small bowl, stir together ranch salad dressing and honey mustard. Set aside.

Wrap bacon in paper towels. Place on a microwave-safe plate. Microwave on high setting (100% power) for 1 minute. Using oven mitts, remove from microwave.

For each wrap, using a table knife, spread 1 tablespoon dressing mixture onto each tortilla. Top with a tomato slice, 2 slices bacon, one-fourth of the chicken strips, and ½ cup lettuce. Tightly roll up tortilla. Have an adult use a sharp knife to cut wraps in half. Serve immediately.

Frenchy au Jus

Start to Finish 20 minutes **Makes** 4 servings

Here's what you do:

1 Preheat oven to 400 degrees F. Place butter in a small bowl; let stand until softened.

2 In a medium saucepan, using a wooden spoon, stir together beef broth and beefy onion soup mix. Place on a burner; turn burner to medium. Bring to simmering; cook for 2 to 3 minutes. Add roast beef to saucepan. Return to simmer. Remove from heat.

3 Separate roll halves. Using a table knife, butter each half and place on baking sheet. Place baking sheet in preheated oven. Bake for 4 to 6 minutes or until toasted. Using oven mitts, remove baking sheet from oven. Transfer roll bottoms to 4 dinner plates.

4 Using tongs, carefully transfer roast beef from broth mixture to a plate. Divide roast beef evenly among French roll bottoms. Top with French roll tops. Using a ladle, spoon some of the broth mixture into 4 small bowls. Place a small bowl on each plate. To eat, dip sandwiches in the broth mixture.

Tools you'll need:

* Small bowl
* Medium saucepan
* Wooden spoon
* Baking sheet
* Oven mitts
* 4 dinner plates
* Tongs
* Plate
* Ladle
* 4 small serving bowls

Food you'll need:

2 tablespoons butter

1 can (14-ounce) reduced-sodium beef broth, *Swanson*®

1 packet (1.1-ounce) beefy onion soup mix, *Lipton*®

1 container (8-ounce) thinly sliced roast beef, *Hillshire Farm*®

4 French rolls, presliced

Cheeseburger Bites

Prep 20 minutes **Bake** 16 minutes **Makes** 16 burgers

Tools you'll need:

* Measuring cups
* Measuring spoons
* Baking sheet
* Aluminum foil
* Large bowl
* Oven mitts
* Wire cooling rack
* Instant-read thermometer
* Cutting board
* 2-inch round cookie cutter
* Sharp knife
* 16 long cocktail toothpicks

Food you'll need:

1 1/4	pounds extra-lean ground beef
1/4	cup ketchup, *Heinz*®
2	tablespoons meat loaf seasoning, *McCormick*®
1	package (7-ounce) sunburst-shape cheese snacks, *Sargento*®
8	hamburger buns, presplit
	Iceberg lettuce leaves
6	tablespoons Thousand Island salad dressing
16	cherry tomatoes
16	pickle chips

Here's what you do:

1 Preheat oven to 375 degrees F. Line baking sheet with aluminum foil; set aside.

2 In a large bowl, mix ground beef, ketchup, and meat loaf seasoning with wet clean hands until well combined. Form into 16 patties slightly larger than 2 inches wide. Place patties on prepared baking sheet. Wash hands well.

3 Place baking sheet in preheated oven. Bake for 14 to 16 minutes. Using oven mitts, remove from oven. Place on a wire rack. Top each patty with a cheese snack. Using oven mitts, return baking sheet to oven. Bake about 2 minutes more or until burgers are done* (160 degrees F) and cheese has melted. Using oven mitts, remove baking sheet from oven. Place on a wire rack.

4 While the burgers cook, arrange halves of hamburger buns on a cutting board, cut sides up. Using a 2-inch round cookie cutter, cut mini buns from the large hamburger buns. Have an adult use a sharp knife to chop lettuce leaves into pieces about 2 inches wide.

5 To assemble cheeseburgers, top bottoms of mini buns with lettuce, a patty, and about 1 teaspoon Thousand Island salad dressing. Add bun tops. Skewer 1 cherry tomato and 1 pickle chip on each of 16 long cocktail toothpicks; push through the centers of assembled burgers.

*Note: For burgers, meatballs, and other pieces of meat, have an adult help you check the temperature with an instant-read thermometer. The meat is done when the temperature reaches the number written in each recipe, such as 160 degrees F (above).

Bacon-Pickle Dogs

Prep 20 minutes Broil 6 minutes Makes 8 sandwiches

Tools you'll need:

* Baking sheet
* Aluminum foil
* Oven-safe wire rack
* Microwave-safe bacon rack
* Paper towels
* Oven mitts
* Fork
* Sharp knife
* Cutting board
* Table knife
* Wooden toothpicks
* Tongs

Food you'll need:

8   slices bacon, *Oscar Mayer*®

4   pickle spears, *Vlasic*®

8   all-beef frankfurters, *Ball Park*®

8   hot dog buns, presplit*

Condiments (such as ketchup and mustard) (optional)

Here's what you do:

Preheat broiler. Line a baking sheet with aluminum foil; position an oven-safe wire rack on top of foil. Set aside.

Place bacon on a microwave-safe bacon rack. Cover with paper towels. Microwave on high setting (100% power) about 1 minute or until edges of slices begin to curl but bacon is still soft. Using oven mitts, remove from microwave. Remove paper towels. Using a fork, transfer bacon to clean paper towels to drain.

Have an adult use a sharp knife to slice each pickle spear lengthwise to make two thinner pieces; set aside. Using a table knife, slice each frankfurter lengthwise but not all the way through. Insert a pickle piece into each frankfurter. Wrap each frankfurter with a bacon slice, securing ends with wooden toothpicks.

Place frankfurters on prepared wire rack on baking sheet. Have an adult place baking sheet under broiler 4 to 6 inches from heat. Broil for 3 to 4 minutes. Have an adult turn frankfurters with tongs. Broil 3 to 4 minutes more or until bacon is crispy. Using oven mitts, remove from oven.

Using tongs, transfer frankfurters to buns. Remove toothpicks. Serve bacon dogs hot with your choice of condiments (optional).

*Note: If you like, have an adult toast buns on a broiler pan under the broiler.

Double Grilled Double Cheese

Start to Finish 20 minutes Makes 4 sandwiches

Here's what you do:

Microwave butter in a microwave-safe bowl covered with plastic wrap on high setting (100% power) for 1 minute or until melted. Using oven mitts, remove from microwave.

Using a pastry brush, lightly butter both sides of 4 bread slices. Place a large skillet on the burner; turn burner to medium-high. Preheat pan until a drop of water sizzles across the surface. Cook buttered bread slices in skillet about 3 to 4 minutes per side or until golden brown (carefully lift bread with a heat-resistant spatula to see if bottom is golden brown). Remove skillet from heat. Using the spatula, transfer bread slices to a wire rack. (These are the center pieces for the sandwiches.)

To build the sandwiches, lay out 4 slices of untoasted bread. Top each bread slice with a slice American cheese and a toasted bread slice. Next add a slice of Monterey Jack cheese; top with remaining untoasted bread slices.

Lightly brush the outside tops and bottoms of sandwiches with some of the melted butter. Place 1 sandwich in skillet. Place skillet on burner. Cook for 3 to 4 minutes over medium-high heat or until bread is golden brown. Using the spatula, very carefully turn sandwich over. Cook for 3 to 4 minutes more or until bread is golden brown and cheese is melted. Using the spatula, transfer sandwich to a dinner plate. Repeat with remaining sandwiches. Serve warm.

Microwave Directions: Toast 12 bread slices in the toaster (do not brush with butter). Assemble sandwiches as directed in step 3, using the toasted bread. Place each sandwich on a microwave-safe plate. Place 1 sandwich in microwave. Cook on high setting (100% power) for 1 minute or until cheese has melted. Repeat with remaining sandwiches.

Tools you'll need:

* Table knife
* Microwave-safe bowl
* Oven mitts
* Plastic wrap
* Pastry brush
* Large skillet
* Heat-resistant spatula
* Wire cooling rack
* Dinner plates

Food you'll need:

2   tablespoons butter

12   slices white sandwich bread, *Sara Lee*®

4   slices American cheese, *Kraft*®

4   slices Monterey Jack cheese, *Kraft*®

Mini Melts

Start to Finish 25 minutes Makes 4 sandwiches

Tools you'll need:

* Small bowl
* Medium bowl
* Fork
* Cutting board
* 3-inch cookie cutters
* Table knife
* Measuring spoons
* Large skillet
* Heat-resistant spatula
* Dinner plates

Food you'll need:

2   to 3 tablespoons butter

2   cans (6 ounces each) water-pack chunk white tuna, StarKist®

3   tablespoons mayonnaise, Hellmann's® or Best Foods®

½   teaspoon salt-free lemon pepper, McCormick®

8   slices white sandwich bread, Sara Lee®

4   slices cheddar cheese, Kraft®

    Canola oil cooking spray, Mazola® Pure

Here's what you do:

Place butter in a small bowl; let stand until softened. In medium bowl, using a fork, combine tuna, mayonnaise, and lemon pepper; set aside.

Place 4 bread slices on a cutting board. Put 1 cheese slice on each bread slice. Place ¼ cup tuna mixture in center of cheese. Place a second bread slice on each sandwich and gently press together.

Using 3-inch cookie cutters, cut sandwiches into fun shapes, such as stars and moons. Using a table knife, spread both sides of sandwiches with softened butter, using about 1 teaspoon butter per side.

Spray a large skillet with cooking spray. Place on burner; turn burner to medium-high. Place 2 sandwiches in skillet. Cook for 3 to 4 minutes or until bread is brown. Using a heat-resistant spatula, carefully turn sandwiches. Cook for 3 to 4 minutes more or until bread is brown and cheese melts. Remove skillet from heat. Using the spatula, transfer each sandwich to a dinner plate. Repeat with remaining sandwiches. Serve warm.

Popcorn Chicken Salad

Here's what you do:

Preheat oven to 425 degrees F. Line a baking sheet with aluminum foil. Place popcorn chicken on baking sheet. Place baking sheet in preheated oven. Bake for 8 to 10 minutes. Using oven mitts, remove baking sheet from oven. Place on wire rack; cool.

For dressing, in a small bowl, using a spoon, stir together ranch salad dressing and barbecue seasoning; set aside.

For salad, tear lettuce into bite-size pieces; measure 8 cups. Place lettuce in a large bowl. Add dressing. Using tongs, toss until lettuce is coated; set aside.

Have an adult use a sharp knife to cut each tomato into 8 wedges and cucumber into 16 slices.

Using tongs, divide lettuce among 4 dinner plates. Place 4 tomato wedges, 4 cucumber slices, and 4 baby carrots on top of lettuce on each plate. Top each salad with one-fourth of the chicken pieces.

Tools you'll need:

* Measuring cups
* Measuring spoons
* Baking sheet
* Aluminum foil
* Oven mitts
* Wire cooling rack
* Small bowl
* Spoon
* Large bowl
* Tongs
* Sharp knife
* Cutting board
* 4 dinner plates

Food you'll need:

1   package (12-ounce) popcorn chicken, *Tyson®*

FOR DRESSING:

1/2 cup ranch salad dressing, *Hidden Valley®*

2   teaspoons barbecue seasoning, *McCormick®*

FOR SALAD:

     Romaine or iceberg lettuce, *Ready Pac®*

2   tomatoes

1   cucumber

16   baby carrots

Teriyaki Noodle Bowl

Start to Finish 20 minutes Makes 4 servings

Tools you'll need:

* Medium microwave-safe bowl
* Oven mitts
* Large cooking pot
* Large spoon
* Ladle
* 4 soup bowls

Food you'll need:

1 package (21-ounce) frozen chicken teriyaki and vegetables complete meal, *Birds Eye® Voila!*

3 cans (14 ounces each) reduced-sodium chicken broth, *Swanson®*

2 packages (3 ounces each) Oriental-flavor ramen noodles, *Top Ramen®*

Here's what you do:

1 Place chicken teriyaki frozen dinner and vegetables in a medium microwave-safe bowl, setting flavor pouch aside. Place in microwave. Cook, uncovered, on high setting (100% power) for 6 minutes. Using oven mitts, remove bowl from microwave.

2 In a large pot, using a large spoon, combine chicken broth and the frozen dinner flavor pouch. Place on burner; turn burner to medium-high. Bring to a boil.

3 Add the heated chicken and vegetables to the pot. Bring back to a boil; set aside seasoning packets for ramen noodles. Add the ramen noodles to the pot. Reduce heat to low; simmer for 3 minutes. Remove pot from heat. Stir in seasoning packets. Using a ladle, divide mixture among 4 soup bowls.

Cheddar Cheese Baked Potato Soup

Start to Finish 25 minutes Makes 6 servings

Here's what you do:

Place potato in microwave. Cook on high setting (100% power) for 7 to 8 minutes. Using oven mitts, carefully remove from microwave. (Potato will be HOT!) Set aside until cool enough to touch. Remove plastic covering.

Have an adult use a sharp knife to cut potato into $\frac{1}{2}$-inch cubes; set aside. In a large saucepan, using a wooden spoon, stir together cheddar cheese soup, chicken broth, and bacon. Place on burner; turn burner to medium. Bring to simmering, stirring occasionally. Stir in potato. Heat and stir soup for 5 minutes. Using a ladle, divide soup among 6 soup bowls. Top each serving with a spoonful of sour cream and a sprinkle of chopped scallion (optional).

Food you'll need:

- 1 potato for the microwave, *Melissa's® Micro Baker Potatoes* (see note, page 107)
- 2 cans (10.75 ounces each) condensed cheddar cheese soup, *Campbell's®*
- 2½ cups reduced-sodium chicken broth, *Swanson®*
- ¼ cup real bacon pieces, *Hormel®*

  Sour cream, *Knudsen®* (optional)
- 1 scallion (green onion), finely chopped (optional)

Dropped Ramen

Start to Finish 15 minutes Makes 4 servings

Here's what you do:

In a medium saucepan, stir together chicken broth and water. Place on a burner; bring to boiling over medium-high heat. Set aside ramen noodle seasoning packet. Stir noodles into boiling broth. Cook for 3 minutes, stirring occasionally.

In a small bowl, beat eggs lightly with a fork. Working with an adult, stir soup while slowly pouring in egg. Remove soup from heat. Continue to stir soup for 1 minute or until egg is evenly distributed and well cooked.

Have an adult use a sharp knife to cut chicken strips into bite-size pieces. Stir chicken pieces and ramen noodle seasoning packet into soup. Divide soup among 4 bowls.

Food you'll need:

- 2 cans (14 ounces each) reduced-sodium chicken broth, *Swanson®*
- 2½ cups water
- 2 packages (3 ounces each) chicken-flavor ramen noodles, *Top Ramen®*
- 2 large eggs
- 1 package (6-ounce) fully cooked chicken strips, *Tyson®*

Meal Mania

Okay, so dinner with the family can be sorta feeble ... unless my nephew Bryce is the chef! At age 6, Bryce is a grade school gourmet, with his own set of cookware and moves that make meals the awesomest. For a long time, Bryce would only eat chicken nuggets. Now he dishes up rad eats like Ritz Sticks and Ranch Slaw and Cowboy Meat Loaf with Glazed Carrots for everyday meals. For special meals, Pineapple Pork Chops cook up quick with Vegetable Fried Rice on the side. And say sayonara to bor-ring, with Pepperoni Chicken and Caesar Pasta on the menu. Clean your plate? No problem!

The Recipes

Ritz Sticks

Prep 25 minutes Bake 10 minutes Makes 4 servings

Tools you'll need:

* Measuring cups
* Measuring spoons
* Baking sheet
* Large zip-top plastic bag
* Rolling pin
* Plate
* Paper towels
* Sharp knife
* Cutting board
* Medium bowl
* Whisk
* Pie plate
* Oven mitts
* Heat-resistant spatula
* 4 dinner plates

Food you'll need:

Canola oil cooking spray,
Mazola® Pure

40 rich round crackers, *Ritz®*

1 pound fresh cod or other firm white fish fillets

1 cup all-purpose flour

2 large eggs

2 tablespoons ranch salad dressing mix, *Hidden Valley®*

2 tablespoons water

Bottled tartar sauce,
Hellmann's® or *Best Foods®*
(optional)

Here's what you do:

1. Preheat oven to 350 degrees F. Lightly spray baking sheet with cooking spray; set aside.

2. Place crackers in a large zip-top plastic bag. Using a rolling pin, crush crackers into very small pieces. Pour crushed crackers onto a plate; set crackers and zip-top bag aside.

3. Rinse fish under cold water; pat dry with paper towels. Have an adult use a sharp knife to cut fish into 1×½-inch strips. In the zip-top plastic bag, combine fish strips and flour. Seal bag; shake to coat fish; set aside.

4. In a medium bowl, using a whisk, combine eggs, ranch salad dressing mix, and water. Pour into a pie plate.

5. Remove fish strips from bag, gently shaking off excess flour. Dip into egg mixture; coat with crushed crackers. Place on prepared baking sheet. Wash hands well.

6. Place baking sheet in preheated oven. Bake for 10 to 12 minutes. Using oven mitts, remove from oven.

7. Using a heat-resistant spatula, transfer fish to 4 dinner plates. Serve with tartar sauce for dipping (optional).

Ranch Slaw

Start to Finish 10 minutes Makes 6 servings

Here's what you do:

In a large bowl, using a wooden spoon, stir together raisins, ranch salad dressing, and sour cream. Add coleslaw mix; toss to combine.

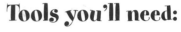

Tools you'll need:

* Measuring cups
* Large bowl
* Wooden spoon

Food you'll need:

$\frac{1}{2}$ cup raisins, *Sun-Maid®*

$\frac{1}{3}$ cup ranch salad dressing, *Hidden Valley®*

$\frac{1}{3}$ cup sour cream, *Knudsen®*

1 bag (16-ounce) tri-color cole slaw mix, *Ready Pac®*

Pepperoni Chicken

Prep 20 minutes Bake 30 minutes Cool 3 minutes Makes 4 servings

Tools you'll need:

* Measuring spoons
* Measuring cups
* Baking sheet
* Aluminum foil
* Cutting board
* Waxed paper
* Meat mallet
* Wooden toothpicks
* Oven mitts
* Wire cooling rack
* Heat-resistant spatula
* 4 dinner plates

Food you'll need:

4   boneless, skinless chicken breast halves

1   teaspoon garlic salt, *Lawry's*®

1   teaspoon dried Italian seasoning, *McCormick*®

$\frac{1}{2}$ cup shredded mozzarella cheese, *Kraft*®

$\frac{1}{4}$ cup diced pepperoni, *Bridgeford*®

Here's what you do:

1 Preheat oven to 350 degrees F. Line a baking sheet with aluminum foil; set aside.

2 Pull the tenders* from each chicken breast half and refrigerate for another use.

3 On a cutting board, place 1 chicken breast half between 2 pieces of waxed paper. Using the smooth side of a meat mallet, pound chicken breast half to $\frac{1}{4}$-inch thickness. Remove from waxed paper. Repeat with remaining chicken breast halves.

4 Sprinkle both sides of each chicken breast half with garlic salt and Italian seasoning. Lay each chicken breast half smooth side down; sprinkle with 2 tablespoons shredded cheese and 1 tablespoon pepperoni.

5 Roll up each chicken breast half. If necessary, secure rolls with wooden toothpicks. Place, seam sides down, on prepared baking sheet. Wash hands well.

6 Place baking sheet in preheated oven. Bake for 30 minutes. Using oven mitts, remove from oven. Place baking sheet on wire rack; cool for 3 minutes. Using a heat-resistant spatula, transfer a chicken breast half to each of 4 dinner plates. Remove toothpicks. Serve warm.

***Note:** If you place the chicken breast half smooth side down, the "tender" is the extra $\frac{1}{2}$-inch-wide piece that runs along one side. Sometimes it is already removed at the store.

Caesar Pasta

Start to Finish 15 minutes Makes 4 servings

Here's what you do:

In a large pot, bring 3 to 4 quarts of water to a boil over high heat. Using a large spoon, stir in pasta; bring back to a boil. Cook for 9 to 10 minutes or until tender, stirring occasionally. Using a colander, have an adult drain pasta and return to pot.

To the pasta, add 1 cup of the Parmesan cheese, the salad dressing, salt, and pepper; toss to combine.

Divide pasta mixture among 4 dinner plates. Serve warm. Sprinkle with more Parmesan cheese (optional).

Tools you'll need:

* Measuring cups
* Measuring spoons
* Large cooking pot
* Large spoon
* Colander
* 4 dinner plates

Food you'll need:

3   to 4 quarts water

8   ounces dried bow tie pasta

1   cup or more shredded Parmesan cheese, *Kraft*®

$\frac{1}{2}$ cup creamy Caesar salad dressing, *Newman's Own*®

$\frac{1}{2}$ teaspoon salt

$\frac{1}{2}$ teaspoon ground black pepper

Chicken Parmesan

Prep 40 minutes Marinate 1 hour Bake 24 minutes Makes 4 servings

Tools you'll need:

* Measuring cups
* 2 large zip-top plastic bags
* Baking sheet
* Aluminum foil
* Oven mitts
* Microwave-safe bowl
* Plastic wrap
* Heat-resistant spatula
* 4 dinner plates
* Spoon

Food you'll need:

4   boneless, skinless chicken breast halves

1   cup Italian salad dressing, *Newman's Own*®

1½ cups Italian seasoned bread crumbs, *Progresso*®

½   cup grated Parmesan cheese, *DiGiorno*®

4   slices mozzarella cheese, *Kraft*®

1   jar (14-ounce) marinara sauce, *Prego*®

Here's what you do:

1. Place chicken breasts and salad dressing in large zip-top plastic bag. Squeeze out excess air from bag and seal. Wash hands well. Gently massage bag to combine ingredients. Place in refrigerator; marinate for 1 to 4 hours. Remove chicken from refrigerator. Let stand at room temperature for 30 minutes.

2. Preheat oven to 350 degrees F. Line baking sheet with aluminum foil; set aside.

3. In another large zip-top plastic bag, combine bread crumbs and Parmesan cheese. Seal bag and shake to mix. Remove chicken from marinade and place in bag with bread crumbs. Discard marinade. Seal bag and shake to coat chicken. Place chicken on prepared baking sheet. Wash hands well. Place baking sheet in preheated oven. Bake for 20 to 25 minutes.

4. Using oven mitts, remove pan from oven. Top each chicken breast with a slice of mozzarella cheese. Return pan to oven. Bake for 4 to 5 minutes more or until cheese is melted. Using oven mitts, remove from oven.

5. Place marinara sauce in microwave-safe bowl. Cover loosely with plastic wrap. Microwave on high setting (100% power) for 3 to 4 minutes or until warm. Using oven mitts, remove from microwave. Carefully remove plastic wrap.

6. Using a heat-resistant spatula, place a chicken breast half on each of 4 dinner plates. Spoon marinara sauce over chicken. Serve immediately.

Pasta Zoo with Peas and Carrots

Start to Finish 25 minutes Makes 4 servings

Here's what you do:

In a large pot, bring 3 to 4 quarts water to a boil over high heat. Using a large spoon, stir in pasta; bring back to a boil. Cook for 10 to 12 minutes or until pasta is tender, stirring occasionally.

Meanwhile, place frozen vegetables in microwave-safe bowl. Cover loosely with plastic wrap. Microwave on high setting (100% power) for 4 to 6 minutes or just until tender. Using oven mitts, remove from microwave. Carefully remove plastic wrap; set aside. Cut butter into 4 pieces.

Using a colander, have an adult drain pasta and return pasta to pot. Add vegetables and butter. Place pot on burner; turn burner to medium. Heat and stir about 3 minutes or until butter is melted. Remove from heat. Season to taste with salt and pepper. Transfer to serving bowl. Serve immediately.

Tools you'll need:

* Measuring spoons
* Large cooking pot
* Large spoon
* Microwave-safe bowl
* Plastic wrap
* Oven mitts
* Table knife
* Colander
* Serving bowl

Food you'll need:

8 ounces dried zoo animal-shape pasta, *Anthony's*®

1½ cups frozen loose-pack peas and carrots, *Birds Eye*®

½ stick (¼ cup) butter

Salt

Ground black pepper

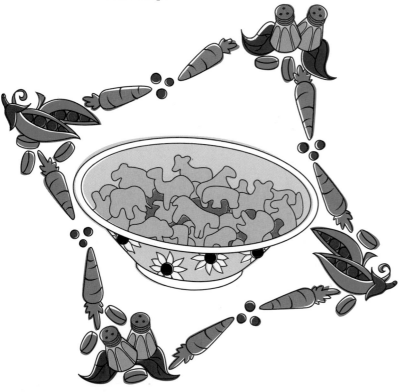

Tex-Mex Baked Turkey Burgers

Prep 20 minutes Bake 21 minutes Makes 4 burgers

Tools you'll need:

* Measuring cups
* Baking sheet
* Aluminum foil
* Large bowl
* Oven mitts
* Cookie cutters
* Heat-resistant spatula
* 4 dinner plates
* Instant-read thermometer

Food you'll need:

1¼ pounds ground raw turkey

¼ cup real bacon pieces, *Hormel*®

¼ cup pasta sauce, *Prego*®

½ packet (half of a 1.25-ounce packet) chili seasoning, *McCormick*®

4 slices cheddar cheese, *Kraft*®

4 slices Monterey Jack cheese, *Kraft*®

Hamburger buns (optional)

Here's what you do:

1. Preheat oven to 400 degrees F. Line a baking sheet with aluminum foil; set aside.

2. In a large bowl, mix turkey, bacon, pasta sauce, and chili seasoning with wet clean hands until well combined. Form mixture into 4 patties. Place on prepared baking sheet. Wash hands well.

3. Place baking sheet in preheated oven. Bake for 20 minutes or until cooked through (165 degrees F; see note, page 40). Meanwhile, using cookie cutters, cut cheese into shapes of your choice.

4. Using oven mitts, remove baking sheet from oven. Top each burger with 1 to 2 cheese shapes. Return pan to oven. Bake for 1 to 2 minutes or until cheese shapes are melted but have not lost their shape. Using oven mitts, remove from oven. Using a heat-resistant spatula, transfer burgers to 4 dinner plates. Serve burgers on buns (optional).

Chili Chips

Prep 5 minutes Bake 25 minutes Makes 4 servings

Here's what you do:

1. Preheat oven to 450 degrees F. Line a baking sheet with aluminum foil.

2. Arrange potatoes in a single layer on baking sheet. Place baking sheet in preheated oven. Bake for 25 minutes. Using oven mitts, remove from oven.

3. Sprinkle hot potatoes with chili seasoning. Using a heat-resistant spatula, toss fries with seasoning. Transfer to a serving bowl. Serve warm.

Tools you'll need:

* Baking sheet
* Aluminum foil
* Oven mitts
* Heat-resistant spatula
* Serving bowl

Food you'll need:

1   package (22-ounce) frozen waffle fries, *Ore-Ida®*

½   packet (half of a 1.25-ounce packet) chili seasoning, *McCormick®*

Pineapple Pork Chops

Prep 20 minutes   Bake 25 minutes   Makes 4 servings

Tools you'll need:

* Measuring spoons
* 13×9-inch baking dish
* Strainer
* Small bowl
* Oven mitts
* Heat-resistant spatula
* 4 dinner plates

Food you'll need:

4   loin pork chops

1   teaspoon garlic salt, *Lawry's*®

1   teaspoon salt-free lemon pepper, *McCormick*®

1   can (8-ounce) pineapple slices, *Dole*®

4   maraschino cherries

4   teaspoons packed light brown sugar, *C&H*®

Here's what you do:

1 Preheat oven to 350 degrees F. Sprinkle both sides of chops with garlic salt and lemon pepper. Put chops in a 13×9-inch baking dish. Wash hands well.

2 Drain pineapple slices; discard liquid. Place a pineapple slice on top of each chop. Place a cherry in the center of each pineapple slice.* Sprinkle each chop with 1 teaspoon brown sugar.

3 Place baking dish in preheated oven. Bake for 25 to 30 minutes. Using oven mitts, remove from oven. Using a heat-resistant spatula, transfer a chop to each of 4 dinner plates.

*Tip: If you like, make a face on your pork chop by placing 2 maraschino cherries on the pineapple slice for eyes. Cut 1 cherry into quarters; use 1 quarter to make a mouth on each pineapple slice. If desired, arrange steamed green beans around the top of the pork chop to resemble hair.

Vegetable Fried Rice

Start to Finish 25 minutes Makes 6 servings

Here's what you do:

In small bowl, using a spoon, stir together stir-fry seasoning and water until seasoning is dissolved; set aside. In a small bowl, using a fork, beat egg lightly.

Place frozen vegetables in a microwave-safe bowl. Cover loosely with plastic wrap. Microwave on high setting (100% power) for 6 minutes. Using oven mitts, remove from microwave. Carefully remove plastic wrap.

Place canola oil in a large skillet. Place on burner; turn burner to medium-high. When oil is hot, pour egg into skillet. Using a spatula, flip one part at a time until all the egg is cooked. Using a wooden spoon, stir in rice, bacon, and cooked vegetables.

Stir seasoning mixture into rice mixture. Cook for 4 to 5 minutes more or until rice is warmed through, stirring occasionally. Transfer to a serving bowl. Serve hot.

Tools you'll need:

* Measuring spoons
* Measuring cups
* 2 small bowls
* Spoon
* Fork
* Microwave-safe bowl
* Plastic wrap
* Oven mitts
* Large skillet
* Heat-resistant spatula
* Wooden spoon
* Serving bowl

Food you'll need:

1   packet (1-ounce) stir-fry seasoning, *Kikkoman*®

2   tablespoons water

1   large egg

8   ounces (half of a 16-ounce bag) frozen stir-fry vegetables, *Birds Eye*®

2   tablespoons canola oil, *Wesson*®

2   packages (8.8 ounces each) chicken-flavor ready rice, *Uncle Ben's*®

1/4 cup real bacon pieces, *Hormel*®

Cowboy Meat Loaf

Prep 10 minutes Bake 50 minutes Cool 5 minutes Makes 4 servings

Tools you'll need:

* Measuring cups
* 11×8-inch baking pan
* Large bowl
* Oven mitts
* Instant-read thermometer
* Wire cooling rack
* Heat-resistant spatula
* Cutting board
* Sharp knife
* 4 dinner plates

Food you'll need:

Canola oil cooking spray, *Mazola® Pure*

1¼ pounds ground raw turkey

½ cup mexicorn, *Green Giant®*

¼ cup precrumbled sharp cheddar cheese, *Kraft®*

1 packet (1.15-ounce) Santa Fe chicken seasoning, *McCormick®*

2 slices bacon, *Oscar Mayer®*

Here's what you do:

1 Preheat oven to 400 degrees F. Spray an 11×8-inch baking pan with cooking spray.

2 In large bowl, mix turkey, mexicorn, cheddar cheese, and chicken seasoning with wet clean hands until well combined. Form into a loaf. Place in prepared baking pan. Crisscross bacon slices on top of turkey loaf. Wash hands well.

3 Place baking pan in oven. Bake for 50 to 55 minutes or until done (165 degrees F; see note, page 40). Using oven mitts, remove from oven. Place on a wire rack; cool for 5 minutes.

4 Have an adult use a heat-resistant spatula to transfer meat loaf to a cutting board; cut meat loaf into slices. Transfer slices to 4 dinner plates. Serve warm.

Glazed Carrots

Start to Finish 20 minutes Makes 4 servings

Here's what you do:

Using a table knife, cut butter into 4 pieces. Place carrots, maple syrup, cinnamon, and butter in a microwave-safe bowl. Cover loosely with plastic wrap. Microwave on high setting (100% power) for 8 minutes. Use oven mitts to remove from microwave. Carefully remove plastic wrap.

Using a spoon, stir mixture. Return to microwave. Cook, uncovered, for 4 minutes, stirring every minute. Using oven mitts, remove from microwave. Serve hot.

Tools you'll need:

* Measuring cups
* Measuring spoons
* Table knife
* Microwave-safe bowl
* Plastic wrap
* Oven mitts
* Spoon

Food you'll need:

$\frac{1}{2}$ stick ($\frac{1}{4}$ cup) butter

2 cups baby carrots

$\frac{1}{4}$ cup pure maple syrup, *Maple Grove Farms*®

$\frac{1}{2}$ teaspoon ground cinnamon, *McCormick*®

Taco Mac

Prep 20 minutes **Bake** 30 minutes **Cool** 5 minutes **Makes** 4 servings

Tools you'll need:

* Measuring cups
* Large skillet
* Wooden spoon
* Oven mitts
* Large bowl
* 3-quart casserole
* Wire cooling rack
* Large spoon
* 4 bowls

Food you'll need:

1   package (14-ounce) macaroni and cheese dinner with four-cheese sauce, *Kraft® Deluxe*

1   pound ground beef

1   packet (1.25-ounce) taco seasoning, *McCormick®*

1   cup tortilla chips, *Tostitos®*

¼   cup shredded Mexican cheese blend, *Kraft®*

Here's what you do:

1 Preheat oven to 350 degrees F. Have an adult help you prepare macaroni and cheese dinner according to package directions; set aside.

2 In a large skillet, using a wooden spoon, stir together ground meat and taco seasoning. Place on burner; turn burner to medium-high. Cook and stir mixture until meat is browned. Remove from heat.

3 In a large bowl, combine macaroni and cheese mixture and meat mixture. Spoon into a 3-quart casserole.

4 Crumble tortilla chips; sprinkle over casserole. Sprinkle with cheese. Place casserole in oven. Bake for 30 minutes. Using oven mitts, remove from oven. Place on a wire rack; cool for 5 minutes. Using a large spoon, transfer to 4 bowls. Serve warm.

Ranchers Salad

Start to Finish 10 minutes Makes 4 servings

Here's what you do:

Have an adult use a sharp knife to chop celery and cut cherry tomatoes in half; set aside.

For dressing, in a small bowl, using a spoon, stir together ranch salad dressing and barbecue seasoning; set aside.

In a medium bowl, combine romaine lettuce, carrots, celery, and cherry tomatoes. Pour dressing over salad. Using two large spoons, toss together to coat lettuce and vegetables. Using tongs, divide salad among 4 salad bowls. Sprinkle with bacon. Serve immediately.

Tools you'll need:

* Measuring cups
* Measuring spoons
* Sharp knife
* Cutting board
* Small bowl
* Spoon
* Medium bowl
* 2 large spoons
* Tongs
* 4 salad bowls

Food you'll need:

1   rib celery

8   cherry tomatoes

1/2   cup ranch salad dressing, *Hidden Valley*®

2   teaspoons barbecue seasoning, *McCormick*®

4   cups torn romaine lettuce, *Ready Pac*®

1   cup baby carrots

1/4   cup real bacon pieces, *Hormel*®

Everyday TV Dinners

When you're 5, cartoons are your life. That and the trampoline. Just ask my nephew, Blake. I have nine nieces and nephews and all the rest of them combined don't have as much energy as Blake. To fuel that hype, Blake wants traditional kid food with a twist—spaghetti topped with chili, meat loaf made into muffins, and lasagna in cool gel pen shades of green and orange. So leave the drama to the cartoon characters—meal prep is no problem with shortcut ingredients like shredded cheese in a bag and canned tomatoes that let even a preschooler help zap up dinner super fast.

The Recipes

Meat Loaf Muffins

Prep 15 minutes Bake 25 minutes Makes 6 servings

Foods you'll need:

Canola oil cooking spray, *Mazola® Pure*

1¼ pounds ground beef

1 packet (1-ounce) onion soup mix, *Lipton®*

½ cup mesquite-flavor barbecue sauce, *Bull's-Eye® Mesquite*

½ cup precrumbled cheddar cheese, *Kraft®*

¼ cup real bacon pieces, *Hormel®*

Here's what you do:

1. Preheat oven to 400 degrees F. Spray the cups of a muffin pan with six 3½-inch cups with cooking spray; set aside.

2. In large bowl, mix ground beef, onion soup mix, ¼ cup of the barbecue sauce, the cheddar cheese, and bacon with wet clean hands until well combined. Shape meat mixture into 6 equal parts; shape into balls. Press into the prepared muffin cups. Top muffins with remaining barbecue sauce.

3. Place muffin pan in preheated oven. Bake for 25 to 30 minutes or until done (160 degrees F; see note, page 40). Using oven mitts, remove from oven. With a knife, loosen edges of meat muffins. Transfer to dinner plates.

Porcupine Meatballs

Prep 30 minutes Cook 20 minutes Makes 6 servings

Foods you'll need:

1½ pounds ground beef

1 cup long grain rice, *Uncle Ben's® Original*

1 large egg

1 packet (1-ounce) onion soup mix, *Lipton®,*

1 can (10.75-ounce) condensed tomato soup, *Campbell's®*

1 can (10.75-ounce) condensed cream of mushroom soup, *Campbell's®*

1 soup can of water

Here's what you do:

1. In large bowl, mix ground beef, ½ cup of the uncooked rice, egg, and 2 tablespoons of the onion soup with wet clean hands until well combined. Form into 2-inch balls.

2. Place remaining rice on a plate. Roll each ball in rice; set aside. Wash hands well.

3. In large saucepan, stir together tomato soup, cream of mushroom soup, water, and the remaining onion soup mix. Place saucepan on a burner; bring to a boil over high heat. Add meatballs; cover. Reduce heat to medium; simmer for 20 to 30 minutes or until meatballs are cooked through (160 degrees F; see note, page 40), stirring occasionally. Remove saucepan from heat. Using a large spoon, divide meatballs among dinner plates. Serve hot.

Hawaiian-Style Burgers

Prep 20 minutes Cook 10 minutes Makes 4 burgers

Here's what you do:

1 In a medium bowl, mix ground beef, onion soup mix, and 1 undrained can of pineapple chunks with wet clean hands until well combined. Form into 4 patties. Place on plate; set aside. Wash hands well.

2 For sauce, in a strainer set over a small bowl, drain the remaining can of pineapple chunks. Discard juice. In a blender, add pineapple chunks and barbecue sauce. Cover; turn on blender. Blend until smooth. Using a rubber spatula, transfer to a serving bowl.

3 Place grill pan or large skillet on burner; turn burner to medium-high. Place patties in grill pan; cook for 5 minutes. Using a heat-resistant spatula, flip patties. Cook for 5 minutes more or until cooked through (160 degrees F; see note, page 40).

4 Have an adult use a serrated knife to split buns in half. Place 1 patty on each bun bottom. Place on dinner plates. Top each patty with some of the sauce and the bun top. Pass the remaining sauce with the burgers.

Tools you'll need:

* Measuring cups
* Medium bowl
* Plate
* Strainer
* Small bowl
* Blender
* Serving bowl
* Grill pan or large skillet
* Heat-resistant spatula
* Instant-read thermometer
* Serrated knife
* Dinner plates

Foods you'll need:

1   pound ground beef

1   packet (1-ounce) onion soup mix, *Lipton®*

2   cans (8 ounces each) pineapple chunks in juice, *Dole®*

1   cup hickory-flavor barbecue sauce, *Bull's-Eye® Sweet Hickory Smoke*

4   hamburger buns, *King's Hawaiian®*

Chili Spaghetti

Prep 10 minutes **Bake** 30 minutes **Makes** 8 servings

Tools you'll need:

* Measuring cups
* Measuring spoons
* 3-quart casserole
* Large cooking pot
* 2 large spoons
* Colander
* Small bowl
* Spoon
* Oven mitts
* Bowls or mugs

Foods you'll need:

Canola oil cooking spray, *Mazola® Pure*

1 pound dried spaghetti, *Barilla®*

2 cans (15 ounces each) turkey chili with no beans, *Hormel®*

1 can (14.5-ounce) diced tomatoes, *Hunt's®*

1 package (8-ounce) precrumbled cheddar and Colby cheese, *Kraft®*

$\frac{1}{4}$ cup plain bread crumbs, *Progresso®*

$\frac{1}{4}$ cup grated Parmesan cheese, *DiGiorno®*

1 tablespoon extra-virgin olive oil, *Bertolli®*

Here's what you do:

1. Preheat oven to 375 degrees F. Lightly spray a 3-quart casserole with cooking spray.

2. In a large pot, bring 4 to 6 quarts water to a boil over high heat. Add spaghetti. Using a large spoon, stir until all of the pasta is covered by water. Bring back to boil; cook about 9 minutes or until pasta is tender, stirring occasionally. Have an adult use a colander to drain pasta and return spaghetti to pot.

3. Stir in chili, undrained tomatoes, and cheese. Transfer to prepared casserole; set aside.

4. In a small bowl, using a spoon, stir together bread crumbs, Parmesan cheese, and olive oil until well mixed. Sprinkle over pasta mixture.

5. Place casserole in preheated oven. Bake for 30 to 35 minutes or until golden brown and heated through. Using oven mitts, remove from oven. Using a large spoon, divide among bowls.

Note: If desired, serve with heart-shape toasted garlic bread.

Sweet & Sour Popcorn Shrimp

Start to Finish 25 minutes Makes 4 servings

Tools you'll need:

* Measuring cups
* 2 medium saucepans
* Spoon
* Baking sheet
* Oven mitts
* Wooden spoon
* Large spoon
* Dinner plates

Foods you'll need:

Hot cooked rice (optional)

10 ounces (half of a 20-ounce package) frozen popcorn shrimp, *Sea Pak®*

1 bottle (11.5-ounce) sweet and sour sauce, *Kikkoman®*

1 can (8-ounce) pineapple chunks, *Dole®*

1 bag (16-ounce) frozen stir-fry vegetables, *Birds Eye®*

Here's what you do:

1 Preheat oven to 450 degrees F. Have an adult help you cook rice (if using) according to package directions; keep warm.

2 Place shrimp in a single layer on baking sheet. Place in preheated oven. Bake for 9 minutes.

3 Meanwhile, in a medium saucepan, using a wooden spoon, stir together sweet and sour sauce, undrained pineapple chunks, and vegetables. Place on burner; turn burner to medium-high. Bring to a boil; reduce to a simmer. Cook and stir for 5 to 7 minutes or until vegetables are tender. Using oven mitts, remove from heat.

4 Using oven mitts, remove shrimp from oven. Stir into vegetable mixture. Using a large spoon, divide hot shrimp mixture among dinner plates. Serve with rice (if using).

Chip Chicken

Prep 10 minutes **Marinate** 1 hour **Bake** 20 minutes
Cool 5 minutes **Makes** 4 servings

Here's what you do:

Place chicken tenders in one of the large zip-top plastic bags. Pour Italian salad dressing over chicken. Place in the refrigerator; marinate for 1 hour. Wash hands well.

Meanwhile, preheat oven to 350 degrees F. Line baking sheet with aluminum foil; set aside. Place several handfuls of plain potato chips in the other large zip-top plastic bag. Using a rolling pin, crush chips into very small pieces; measure 1 cup (if you don't have enough to equal 1 cup, crush another handful). Place in a shallow bowl; set aside. Place several handfuls of barbecue potato chips in the zip-top plastic bag, Using the rolling pin, crush chips into very small pieces; measure 1 cup. Place in another shallow bowl.

Using a slotted spoon, remove chicken from marinade. Place chicken tenders on a large plate. Discard marinade. Working with 1 chicken tender at a time, press half the chicken tenders into the plain potato chips, coating both sides. Press the other half of the tenders into the barbecue potato chips, coating both sides. Arrange chicken tenders on the prepared baking sheet. Wash hands well.

Place baking sheet in preheated oven. Bake for 20 to 25 minutes. Using oven mitts, remove from oven. Cool for 5 minutes. Divide chicken tenders among dinner plates. Serve ranch dressing with chicken tenders.

Tools you'll need:

* Measuring cups
* 2 large zip-top plastic bags
* Baking sheet
* Aluminum foil
* Rolling pin
* 2 shallow bowls
* Slotted spoon
* Large plate
* Oven mitts
* Dinner plates

Foods you'll need:

1 1/4 pounds chicken tenders

3/4 cup Italian salad dressing, *Newman's Own*®

Plain potato chips, *Lay's*®

Barbecue potato chips, *Lay's*®

Ranch salad dressing, *Hidden Valley*®

Taco Rice Bowl

Start to Finish 30 minutes Makes 4 servings

Tools you'll need:

* Measuring cups
* Sharp knife
* Cutting board
* Measuring spoons
* Medium saucepan
* Wooden spoon
* Fork
* Large spoon
* 4 bowls

Foods you'll need:

   Lettuce

1   scallion (green onion) (optional)

1   can (14.5-ounce) diced tomatoes, *Hunt's*®

1½ cups water

1   packet (1.25-ounce) taco seasoning, *McCormick*®

2   cups instant rice, *Uncle Ben's*®

2   packages (6 ounces each) grilled chicken breast strips, *Tyson*®

1   cup precrumbled cheddar cheese, *Kraft*®

¼   cup sour cream, *Knudsen*®

Here's what you do:

1 With your hands, shred lettuce into bite-size pieces. Measure 1 cup of lettuce; set aside. Have an adult use a sharp knife to chop scallion; set aside.

2 In a medium saucepan, using a wooden spoon, stir together undrained tomatoes, water, and taco seasoning. Place on burner; turn burner to medium-high. Bring to a boil. Stir in rice; cover. Remove from heat. Let stand 8 to 10 minutes or until all the liquid is absorbed. Using a fork, fluff rice.

3 To serve, using a large spoon, divide rice among 4 bowls. Top each with half of a package chicken strips, ¼ cup cheese, ¼ cup shredded lettuce, and 1 tablespoon sour cream. Sprinkle chopped scallion on top (optional).

Cheesy Chicken Enchiladas

Prep 20 minutes Bake 40 minutes Makes 8 servings

Here's what you do:

Preheat oven to 350 degrees F. In a strainer set over a small bowl, drain green chiles. Discard liquid; transfer chiles to the bowl; set aside. In the same strainer set over another small bowl, drain olives; set aside. Discard liquid.

Spoon beans into a microwave-safe bowl. Cover loosely with plastic wrap. Place in microwave. Cook on high setting (100% power) for 2 minutes. Using oven mitts, remove from microwave. Carefully remove plastic wrap. Measure ¼ cup enchilada sauce. Stir into beans; set aside.

In a large bowl, stack tortillas. Pour remaining enchilada sauce over tortillas.

With clean hands, layer 4 tortillas on the bottom of a 3-quart casserole. Tear tortillas to fit to edge of dish. Top with half of the beans, the contents of 1 package of chicken strips, 1 cup of the cheese, and half of the green chiles. Repeat layers once more.

Place remaining tortillas on top of last layer of filling and pour any remaining enchilada sauce over tortillas. Sprinkle remaining cheese on top. Sprinkle with olives.

Place casserole in preheated oven. Bake for 40 to 45 minutes. Using oven mitts, remove from oven. Using a large spoon, divide enchiladas among dinner plates. Serve hot.

Tools you'll need:

* Measuring cups
* Strainer
* 2 small bowls
* Spoon
* Microwave-safe bowl
* Plastic wrap
* Large bowl
* 3-quart casserole
* Oven mitts
* Large spoon
* Dinner plates

Foods you'll need:

1	can (4-ounce) diced green chiles, *Ortega®*
1	can (2.25-ounce) sliced black olives, *Early California®*
1	can (16-ounce) refried black beans, *Rosarita®*
1	can (15-ounce) red or green enchilada sauce, *Hatch®*
1	bag (14-ounce) corn tortillas, *Mission®*
2	packages (6 ounces each) fully cooked chicken breast strips, *Tyson®*
3	cups shredded Mexican cheese blend, *Kraft®*

Baked Chicken Pasta

Prep 15 minutes Bake 35 minutes Stand 5 minutes Makes 8 servings

Tools you'll need:

* Measuring cups
* Measuring spoons
* Large cooking pot
* Colander
* Strainer
* Small bowl
* Wooden spoon
* 13×9-inch baking dish
* Medium bowl
* Spoon
* Oven mitts
* Large spoon
* Dinner plates

Foods you'll need:

1   pound dried elbow macaroni, *Barilla*®

1   can (2.25-ounce) sliced black olives, *Early California*®

1   jar (16-ounce) Alfredo sauce, *Classico*®

1   can (14.5-ounce) diced tomatoes, *Del Monte*®

2   packages (6 ounces each) cooked chicken breast strips, *Louis Rich*®

$\frac{1}{2}$ cup half-and-half

$\frac{1}{2}$ cup Italian-seasoned bread crumbs, *Progresso*®

2   tablespoons extra-virgin olive oil, *Bertolli*®

Here's what you do:

1. Preheat oven to 350 degrees F. In a large pot over high heat, have an adult bring water to a boil. Add pasta; bring back to a boil. Cook for 10 to 12 minutes or until pasta is tender, stirring occasionally. Have an adult drain pasta in a colander and return to pot.

2. While pasta is cooking, in a strainer set over a small bowl, drain olives; set aside. Discard liquid.

3. To the pasta, add Alfredo sauce, undrained tomatoes, chicken strips, half-and-half, and olives. Using a wooden spoon, stir ingredients together. Place mixture in 13×9-inch baking dish; set aside.

4. In medium bowl, using a spoon, stir together bread crumbs and olive oil until well mixed. Sprinkle over pasta mixture.

5. Place baking dish in preheated oven. Bake for 35 to 40 minutes. Using oven mitts, remove from oven. Cool for 5 minutes. Using a large spoon, divide casserole among dinner plates.

Green and Orange Lasagna

Prep 25 minutes Bake 50 minutes Cool 5 minutes Makes 12 servings

Here's what you do:

Preheat oven to 350 degrees F. Place carrots and 1 tablespoon of the water in microwave-safe bowl. Cover with plastic wrap. Microwave on high setting (100% power) for 6 minutes. Remove from microwave; cool slightly. In a strainer, drain carrots. Transfer carrots to a bowl.

Place spinach and remaining water in the microwave-safe bowl. Cover with plastic wrap. Microwave on high setting (100% power) for 6 minutes. Remove from microwave; cool. Drain spinach in the strainer. When cool, squeeze as much liquid as possible out of spinach; set aside.

Place half of the ricotta cheese, 1 egg, and 1 teaspoon of the Italian seasoning in a blender. Add drained carrots. Cover; turn on blender. Blend until smooth. Using a rubber spatula, transfer carrot mixture to a bowl. Rinse out blender. Place remaining ricotta cheese, 1 egg, and Italian seasoning in blender. Add spinach. Cover; turn on blender. Blend until smooth

Pour half a jar of Alfredo sauce in the bottom of 15×10-inch baking dish. Tilt pan to coat bottom. Add 1 layer of dry noodles. Spread carrot mixture over noodles. Sprinkle 1 cup Italian cheese blend on top. Spoon another half a jar of Alfredo sauce over cheese. Add another layer of dry noodles; repeat layers using spinach mixture, 1 cup of cheese blend, and half a jar of Alfredo sauce. Add a layer of noodles; top with remaining Alfredo sauce and cheese.

Cover baking dish with aluminum foil. Place in preheated oven. Bake for 35 to 40 minutes. Using oven mitts, remove from oven. Remove foil. Return baking dish to oven. Bake for 15 to 20 minutes more or until cheese is bubbling and starting to brown. Using oven mitts, remove from oven. Cool 5 minutes. Cut into squares. Serve warm.

Tools you'll need:

* Measuring cups
* Measuring spoons
* 2 microwave-safe bowls
* Plastic wrap
* Oven mitts
* Strainer
* 2 small bowls
* Blender
* 15×10-inch baking dish
* Aluminum foil
* Heat-resistant spatula

Foods you'll need:

2 cups shredded carrots, *Ready Pac®*

2 tablespoons water

1 package (9-ounce) frozen chopped spinach, *Birds Eye®*

1 container (32-ounce) part-skim ricotta cheese, *Precious®*

2 large eggs

2 teaspoons dried Italian seasoning, *McCormick®*

2 jars (16 ounces each) roasted garlic Alfredo sauce, *Classico®*

1 box (1-pound) no-boil lasagna noodles, *Anthony®*

3 cups shredded Italian cheese blend, *Kraft®*

Brainiac Breaks

It's true—when I was in school, I needed a little incentive to hit the books. Not so with my nephew, Brandon, who makes great grades and aces baseball and football too. At 13, Brandon has learned that whipping up winning snacks is a smart way to score points, whether it's after sports, after school, or after whatever. Big test tomorrow? Groovy smoothies make a mindblowing study buddy ... or you could just wing it with Wild Teriyaki Wings. Chalk up an A for artistic with Nacho Potatoes or bake 'n' take Soft Pretzels for a postpractice pick-me-up. Snack attack? No way! Crack open the cookbook and batter up, then eat up the attention.

The Recipes

Wild Teriyaki Wings

Prep 25 minutes Marinate 1 hour Bake 40 minutes Makes 6 servings

Tools you'll need:

* Measuring spoons
* Measuring cups
* Baking sheet
* Aluminum foil
* Large zip-top plastic bag
* Oven mitts
* Tongs
* Serving plate
* 2 small bowls
* 2 spoons
* Plastic wrap

Food you'll need:

3   pounds chicken drumettes, *Foster Farms*®

1   tablespoon salt

1   teaspoon ground black pepper

1   bottle (10-ounce) teriyaki marinade, *Kikkoman*®

1   can (8-ounce) crushed pineapple, *Dole*®

2   tablespoons sesame seeds (optional)

1   recipe Veggie Dipping Sauce

1   recipe Peanut Dipping Sauce

Here's what you do:

1 Preheat oven to 400 degrees F. Line a baking sheet with aluminum foil; set aside.

2 Season chicken drumettes with salt and pepper. Place chicken in a large zip-top plastic bag. Pour teriyaki marinade and undrained crushed pineapple into the bag. Wash hands well. Squeeze excess air from bag and seal. Gently massage ingredients in bag to combine. Place bag in refrigerator; marinate for 1 hour.

3 Remove drumettes from bag. Discard marinade. Arrange drumettes evenly on prepared baking sheet. Wash hands.

4 Place baking sheet in preheated oven. Bake for 40 minutes or until cooked through. Using oven mitts, remove from oven. Using tongs, place drumettes on a serving plate. Sprinkle with sesame seeds (optional). Serve with Veggie Dipping Sauce and Peanut Dipping Sauce.

Veggie Dipping Sauce: In a small bowl, using a spoon, combine 1 container (8-ounce) light garden vegetable cream cheese, *Philadelphia*®, and 1 cup sour cream, *Knudsen*®. Cover with plastic wrap. Chill in the refrigerator until ready to serve. Makes 2 cups.

Peanut Dipping Sauce: In a small bowl, using a spoon, combine 1 cup creamy peanut butter, *Laura Scudder's*®, 1 cup plain yogurt, *Dannon*®, and 2 tablespoons frozen limeade concentrate, thawed, *Minute Maid*®. Cover with plastic wrap. Chill in the refrigerator until ready to serve. Makes 2 cups.

Turkey Wheels

Start to Finish 10 minutes Makes 4 servings

Here's what you do:

Using a table knife, spread 2 tablespoons cream cheese on each tortilla. On one half of each tortilla, add ½ cup lettuce and one-fourth of the turkey slices. Sprinkle with 2 tablespoons shredded carrots.

Fold in the sides of each tortilla. Starting from the edge where you placed the turkey, roll up tortilla.

Using a serrated knife, have an adult help you cut each roll into 1-inch slices. Transfer to a serving plate.

*Note: For bright, colorful Turkey Wheels, use green spinach and/or red sun-dried tomato tortillas.

Tools you'll need:

* Measuring cups
* Table knife
* Serrated knife
* Serving plate

Food you'll need:

½ cup light garden vegetable-flavor cream cheese, *Philadelphia*®

4 wrap-size (10-inch) flour tortillas,* *Mission*®

2 cups torn mixed greens, *Earthbound Farm*®

1 package (8-ounce) turkey breast slices, *Healthy Choice*®

½ cup shredded carrots, *Ready Pac*®

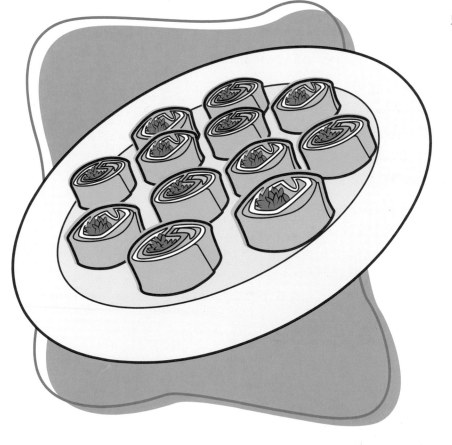

Ham and Cheese Pockets

Prep 20 minutes **Bake** 15 minutes **Cool** 10 minutes **Makes** 8 pockets

Tools you'll need:

* Measuring spoons
* Measuring cups
* Baking sheet
* Aluminum foil
* Small bowl
* Fork
* Rolling pin
* Spoon
* Pastry brush
* Oven mitts
* Heat-resistant spatula
* Wire cooling rack

Food you'll need:

1   egg

1   tablespoon milk

2   tablespoons all-purpose flour

1   can (16.3-ounce) refrigerated cheddar biscuits, *Pillsbury® Grands!*

1   can (10.75-ounce) condensed cheddar cheese soup, *Campbell's®*

1   package (8-ounce) shredded cheddar cheese, *Kraft®*

1/2   cup diced ham, *Hormel®*

Here's what you do:

1. Preheat oven to 350 degrees F. Line a baking sheet with aluminum foil; set aside. In a small bowl, using a fork, beat together egg and milk; set aside.

2. Sprinkle some of the flour onto a flat surface and onto a rolling pin. Roll each biscuit to make a 5-inch circle, turning the biscuit with each roll so it doesn't stick. (If dough starts to stick, sprinkle more flour on the rolling surface.)

3. To make each pocket, using a spoon, spread 1 teaspoon cheddar cheese soup in the center of each biscuit. Top with 1 tablespoon cheese and 1 tablespoon ham. Using a pastry brush, brush a little of the egg mixture around the outside of the circle. Fold biscuit over to form a half circle. Pinch edges together to seal.

4. Evenly space pockets on prepared baking sheet. Brush each pocket with a thin layer of egg mixture

5. Place baking sheet in oven. Bake for 15 to 18 minutes. Using oven mitts, remove from oven. Using a heat-resistant spatula, transfer to wire rack; cool about 10 minutes or until warm to touch.

Power Burritos

Start to Finish 15 minutes Makes 4 burritos

Here's what you do:

1 Spoon beans into microwave-safe bowl. Cover loosely with plastic wrap. Place in microwave. Cook on high setting (100% power) for 2 or 3 minutes or until just warm. Using oven mitts, remove beans from microwave. Carefully remove plastic wrap.

2 Using a spoon, spread $\frac{1}{4}$ cup beans in the center of each tortilla. Top each with half a package of chicken, $\frac{1}{4}$ cup shredded cheese, and $1\frac{1}{2}$ tablespoons salsa.

3 Fold two sides of the tortilla into the center and hold them in place. Starting with the edge closest to you, roll up the tortilla, keeping all the filling inside.

4 Place 2 burritos on a microwave-safe plate. Cover with a paper towel. Place in the microwave. Cook on high setting (100% power) for 2 to 3 minutes. Using oven mitts, remove from microwave. Let cool slightly. Repeat process with remaining burritos.

Tools you'll need:

* Measuring cups
* Measuring spoons
* Spoon
* Microwave-safe bowl
* Plastic wrap
* Oven mitts
* Microwave-safe plate
* Paper towels

Food you'll need:

1 cup low-fat black beans or refried beans, *Rosarita®*

4 burrito-size (10-inch) flour tortillas, *Mission®*

2 packages (6 ounce each) grilled chicken breast strips, *Louis Rich®*

1 cup shredded Mexican cheese blend, *Kraft®*

6 tablespoons mild chunky salsa, *Pace®*

Pizza Braids

Prep 20 minutes Bake 12 minutes Cool 10 minutes Makes 4 braids

Tools you'll need:

* Measuring cups
* Measuring spoons
* Baking sheet
* Aluminum foil
* Small bowl
* Fork
* 2 plates
* Pastry brush
* Oven mitts
* Heat-resistant spatula
* Wire cooling rack
* Microwave-safe bowl
* Plastic wrap

Food you'll need:

1   large egg

1   tablespoon milk

¾   cup diced pepperoni, *Hormel®*

¼   cup grated Parmesan cheese, *DiGiorno®*

1   can (11-ounce) refrigerated breadsticks, *Pillsbury®*

1   teaspoon dried Italian seasoning, *McCormick®*

     Pizza sauce, *Enrico's®*

Here's what you do:

1 Preheat oven to 375 degrees F. Line a baking sheet with aluminum foil. In a small bowl, beat together egg and milk with a fork; set aside. Spread pepperoni on 1 plate; spread Parmesan cheese onto another plate. Set both aside.

2 Separate breadstick dough into 12 individual pieces. Place on a cutting board. Using a pastry brush, brush a thin coating of egg mixture over dough pieces.

3 Place 1 breadstick into pepperoni on the plate, pressing so pepperoni sticks to dough. Repeat with 3 breadsticks for a total of 4 pepperoni-covered breadstick pieces. Press 4 more bread sticks into cheese, pressing so cheese sticks to dough. Sprinkle the remaining 4 breadsticks with Italian seasoning.

4 To make braids, place 1 breadstick with pepperoni, 1 breadstick with cheese, and 1 breadstick with Italian seasoning ¼ inch apart on a flat surface. Starting at the top, intertwine the 3 breadsticks to form a braid. Place braids 1 inch apart on prepared baking sheet.

5 Place baking sheet in preheated oven. Bake for 12 to 14 minutes. Using oven mitts, remove from oven. Using a heat-resistant spatula, transfer to wire rack; cool for 10 minutes.

6 Meanwhile, place pizza sauce in a microwave-safe bowl. Cover loosely with plastic wrap. Microwave on high setting (100% power) for 1 to 1½ minutes or until heated through. Using oven mitts, remove from microwave. Remove plastic wrap. Serve braids with pizza sauce for dipping.

Nacho Potatoes

Start to Finish 35 minutes Makes 4 servings

Tools you'll need:

* Measuring spoons
* Measuring cups
* Baking sheet
* Aluminum foil
* Strainer
* Small bowl
* Oven mitts
* Spoon
* Microwave-safe bowl
* Plastic wrap
* Microwave-safe plate

Food you'll need:

I	can (2.25-ounce) sliced black olives, *Early California*®
II	ounces (half of a 22-ounce bag) waffle fries, *Ore-Ida*®
I	can (16-ounce) refried black beans, *Rosarita*®
I	cup Mexican cheese blend, *Kraft*®
1/2	cup mild chunky salsa, *Pace*®
1/2	cup sour cream, *Knudsen*®

Here's what you do:

1 Preheat oven to 400 degrees F. Line a baking sheet with aluminum foil; set aside. Using a strainer set over a small bowl, drain olives; set aside. Discard liquid.

2 Arrange fries in a single layer on prepared baking sheet. Place baking sheet in preheated oven. Bake for 18 to 20 minutes. Using oven mitts, remove from oven.

3 While fries are baking, spoon black beans into a microwave-safe bowl. Cover bowl loosely with plastic wrap. Place in microwave. Cook on high setting (100% power) for 4 to 6 minutes. Using oven mitts, remove from microwave. Cool about 5 minutes. Carefully remove plastic wrap.

4 To assemble, evenly space fries on a microwave-safe plate. Top each with 1 tablespoon beans, a sprinkling of cheese, and a few olives. Place in microwave. Cook, uncovered, on high setting (100% power) for 1 minute or until cheese melts. Using oven mitts, remove from microwave.

5 Top each stack with about 1 teaspoon salsa and 1 teaspoon sour cream. Serve immediately.

Chili Tots

Here's what you do:

1 Preheat oven to 375 degrees F. Arrange potatoes in a single layer on the bottom of a 9-inch glass pie plate. Using a wooden spoon, spread chili over potatoes.

2 With a table knife, cut frankfurters into 1-inch pieces; place over chili. Sprinkle cheese over frankfurters.

3 Place pie plate in preheated oven. Bake for 40 to 45 minutes or until potatoes are tender and mixture is heated through. Using oven mitts, remove from oven. Cool for 3 to 5 minutes.

Tools you'll need:

* Measuring cups
* 9-inch glass pie plate
* Wooden spoon
* Table knife
* Oven mitts

Food you'll need:

16 ounces (half of a 32-ounce bag) tater tots, *Ore-Ida*®

1 can (15-ounce) turkey chili, *Hormel*®

4 turkey frankfurters, *Ball Park*®

$\frac{2}{3}$ cup shredded cheddar cheese, *Kraft*®

Soft Pretzels

Prep 25 minutes **Rise** 30 minutes **Bake** 12 minutes per batch **Makes** 12 pretzels

Tools you'll need:

* Measuring cups
* Measuring spoons
* 2 baking sheets
* 2 small bowls
* Spoon
* Fork
* Table knife
* Dish towel
* Ruler
* Pastry brush
* Oven mitts
* Heat-resistant spatula
* Wire cooling rack

Food you'll need:

Butter-flavor cooking spray, *Mazola® Pure*

2   teaspoons baking soda

1   cup hot water

1   large egg

3   loaves (1 pound each) frozen white bread dough, thawed, *Bridgford®*

All-purpose flour

TOPPINGS (OPTIONAL):

Sesame seeds

Grated Parmesan cheese, *DiGiorno®*

Cinnamon-sugar mix, *McCormick®*

Kosher salt

Here's what you do:

1. Generously spray 2 baking sheets with cooking spray; set aside.

2. In a small bowl, using a spoon, stir baking soda into hot water until baking soda is dissolved; set aside. In another small bowl, using a fork, beat together egg and 1 teaspoon cold *water;* set aside.

3. Using a table knife, cut each bread loaf into 4 even pieces, making a total of 12 pieces. Lightly sprinkle a flat surface with flour. Roll each dough piece into a rope 36 inches long. (Keep the unused dough covered with a clean dish towel to prevent it from drying out.)

4. Form ropes into pretzel shapes. Place pretzels about 1½ inches apart on prepared baking sheets (if necessary, spray more baking sheets). Using a pastry brush, brush with baking soda mixture. Set aside; let dough rise for 30 minutes.

5. Preheat oven to 450 degrees F. Using a pastry brush, brush pretzels with egg mixture and sprinkle with desired toppings (optional). Place one baking sheet in preheated oven. Bake for 12 or 15 minutes per batch or until well browned. Using oven mitts, remove from oven. Using a heat-resistant spatula, transfer to a wire rack; cool slightly. Serve warm.*

*__Tip:__ For an additional treat, brush pretzels with melted butter before eating.

Nuts and Stuff

Start to Finish 5 minutes Makes 5 cups

Here's what you do:

In a medium bowl, using a wooden spoon, stir together peanuts, cherries, cranberries, and blueberries. Stir in raisins (optional). Serve immediately or store in a large zip-top plastic bag.

Tip: Try Nuts and Stuff on hot cereal such as oatmeal.

Food you'll need:

- 1   can (12-ounce) dry roasted peanuts, *Planters®*
- 1   package (6-ounce) dried cherries, *Mariani®*
- 1   package (5-ounce) dried cranberries, *Sunsweet®*
- 1   package (3-ounce) dried blueberries, *Mariani®*
- 1   package (8.5-ounce) chocolate-covered raisins, *Planters®* (optional)

Veggie Sticks & Cheddar Ranch Dip

Start to Finish 10 minutes Makes 2 cups

Here's what you do:

In a medium bowl, using a wooden spoon, stir together sour cream, cheese dip, and ranch salad dressing mix. Transfer dip to a serving bowl. Serve dip with carrot and celery sticks.

Food you'll need:

- 1   cup sour cream, *Knudsen®*
- 1   cup cheese dip, *Tostitos® Salsa con Queso*
- 1   envelope (1-ounce) ranch salad dressing mix, *Hidden Valley®*
- 1   container (14-ounce) precut carrot and celery sticks, *Ready Pac®*

BLT Dip

Start to Finish 15 minutes **Makes** 2 cups dip

Tools you'll need:

* Measuring cups
* Sharp knife
* Cutting board
* 2 small bowls
* Strainer
* Medium bowl
* Spoon
* Serving plate

Food you'll need:

1   package (12-ounce) whole wheat pita bread rounds, *Sara Lee*®

1   head iceberg lettuce

½   cup sun-dried tomatoes

1   cup sour cream, *Knudsen*®

¾   cup mayonnaise, *Hellmann's*® or *Best Foods*®

½   cup real bacon pieces, *Hormel*®

    Salt and ground black pepper

Here's what you do:

1 Have an adult use a sharp knife to accomplish the following tasks: Cut the pita bread rounds into triangles, cut the core from lettuce head to form a bowl, and chop the dried tomatoes. Set everything aside except the tomatoes.

2 In a small bowl, cover tomatoes with warm water. Let stand about 5 minutes or until softened. Using a strainer set over a small bowl, drain. Discard liquid

3 For the dip, in medium bowl, using a spoon, stir together sour cream, mayonnaise, bacon, and tomatoes. Season with salt and pepper.

4 Spoon dip into hollowed-out lettuce head.* Place in the center of a serving plate. Arrange pita bread triangles around the edge of the plate.

*Tip: If you like, make a cat face in the dip. For the mouth, reserve a piece of lettuce from the removed core of the lettuce bowl. For the nose and eyes, use 3 large pieces of meaty bacon pieces. For the whiskers, use two fresh chives on each cheek. For the ears, insert 2 pita bread triangles at the top of the face. Meow!

Oatmeal Energy Bars

Prep 20 minutes Bake 20 minutes Cool 20 minutes Makes 10 bars

Tools you'll need:

* Measuring cups
* 11×7-inch or 9×9-inch baking pan
* Small bowl
* Fork
* Medium bowl
* Wooden spoon
* Oven mitts
* Wire cooling rack
* Table knife

Food you'll need:

  Canola oil cooking spray, *Mazola® Pure*

1 large egg

¾ cup baking mix, *Bisquick®*

2 cups quick-cooking oats, *Quaker®*

½ cup creamy peanut butter, *Skippy®*

½ cup cinnamon applesauce, *Mott's®*

⅓ cup honey, *SueBee®*

½ cup raisins, *Sun-Maid®*

½ cup semisweet or milk chocolate pieces, *Nestlé®*

Here's what you do:

1 Preheat oven to 350 degrees F. Lightly spray an 11×7-inch or 9×9-inch baking pan with cooking spray; set aside. In a small bowl, using a fork, beat egg lightly.

2 In a medium bowl, using a wooden spoon, stir together baking mix and oats until well blended. Stir in peanut butter, applesauce, and honey until well combined. Stir in raisins and chocolate pieces.

3 Press dough into prepared baking pan. Using oven mitts, place baking pan in preheated oven. Bake for 20 to 25 minutes. Using oven mitts, remove from oven. Place on wire rack; cool about 20 minutes or until completely cool. With a table knife, cut into bars.

Talkin' Trail Mix

Prep 10 minutes **Bake** 8 minutes **Cool** 10 minutes **Makes** 3 cups

Here's what you do:

1 Preheat oven to 350 degrees F. Line a baking sheet with aluminum foil.

2 Evenly spread almonds, pumpkin seeds, and coconut on prepared baking sheet. Place baking sheet in oven. Bake for 8 to 10 minutes or until you begin to smell the nuts and coconut toasting and they are lightly browned. Using oven mitts, carefully remove from oven. Place on wire rack; cool about 10 minutes or until completely cool.

3 In a large bowl, using a large spoon, stir together almond mixture, cranberries, and chocolate pieces. Serve immediately or store in a large zip-top plastic bag.

Tools you'll need:

* Measuring cups
* Baking sheet
* Aluminum foil
* Oven mitts
* Wire cooling rack
* Large bowl
* Large spoon
* Large zip-top plastic bag

Food you'll need:

1 bag (6-ounce) slivered almonds, *Planters*®

½ cup shelled pumpkin seeds (pepitas)

½ cup shredded coconut, *Baker's*®

½ cup dried cranberries, *Ocean Spray*®

½ cup milk chocolate pieces, *Nestlé*®

Smoothie Pops

Prep 10 minutes Freeze 6 hours Makes 8 pops

Tools you'll need:

* Measuring cups
* Measuring spoons
* Blender
* Rubber spatula
* Spoon
* Frozen pop stick molds or paper cups and wooden lollipop sticks
* Plastic wrap

Food you'll need:

3   containers (6 ounces each) low-fat vanilla yogurt, *Dannon*®

1   cup frozen loose-pack mixed berries, *C&W*®

1/4 teaspoon coconut extract, *McCormick*®

Here's what you do:

1 In blender, add yogurt, berries, and coconut extract. Cover; turn on blender. Pulse (start and stop) the blender several times until thoroughly mixed, leaving the berries a little chunky. If necessary, turn off the blender and scrape blender sides with a rubber spatula.

2 Spoon yogurt mixture into frozen pop stick molds,* leaving 1/4-inch space at the top of each mold. Put on tops of frozen pop stick molds. Freeze for at least 6 hours.

3 To serve, run molds under warm water for a few seconds. Grab frozen pop stick and gently pull. Serve immediately.

*Note: If you don't have frozen pop stick molds, pour 1/4 cup of the yogurt mixture into each of 8 small paper cups, *Dixie*®. Cover with plastic wrap and poke a wooden lollipop stick through the plastic into the center of each cup. Freeze as directed.

P.B. Smoothie

Start to Finish 5 minutes Makes 2 (8-ounce) servings

Here's what you do:

1 Using a table knife, cut banana into slices. Pour milk into a blender. Add yogurt, peanut butter, and sliced banana. Cover; turn on blender. Blend for 20 to 30 seconds or until well mixed. If necessary, turn off the blender and scrape sides with a rubber spatula.

2 Pour into 2 large glasses. Serve with straws.

Tools you'll need:

* Measuring cups
* Table knife
* Blender
* 2 large glasses
* 2 straws

Food you'll need:

1   small banana

1   cup milk

¼   cup creamy peanut butter, *Laura Scudder's®*

1   container (6-ounce) banana yogurt, *Yoplait® Original*

Strawberry Energizer

Start to Finish 5 minutes Makes 2 (8-ounce) servings

Here's what you do:

1 Place strawberry nectar in blender. Add frozen strawberries and yogurt. Cover; turn on blender. Blend for 30 to 60 seconds or until smooth. If necessary, turn off the blender and scrape sides with a rubber spatula.

2 Pour into 2 large glasses. Serve immediately.

Tools you'll need:

* Measuring cups
* Blender
* 2 large glasses

Food you'll need:

6   ounces (about half an 11.5-ounce can) strawberry nectar, *Kerns®*

1   cup frozen whole strawberries, *Dole®*

1   container (6-ounce) nonfat strawberry yogurt, *Dannon®*

Movie Munchies

When my nephew, Austen, isn't snowboarding a halfpipe or hitting a homerun, he hangs out at the movies. Or he fires up the DVD and brings the movies to him. A movie without munchies? LOL! It's hard to top popcorn, but Austen's Popcorn Nachos just might do it. Pizza Dogs make a quick flick food, so heat up the toppings before the credits begin. It's all Mission Possible with a microwave. Next stop, nirvana, with you-do-it treats like Triple Chocolate Ice Cream Sandwiches and Funtastic Fruit Leather. For these hook-ups, forks are so not cool—they'll fly right off the plate.

The Recipes

Parmesan Popcorn & Pretzel Sticks

Start to Finish 10 minutes Makes 6 cups

Tools you'll need:

* Large bowl
* Large spoon
* Small microwave-safe bowl
* Plastic wrap
* Oven mitts

Food you'll need:

4   cups popped popcorn

2   cups pretzel sticks, *Rold Gold*®

1   tablespoon butter

¾   cup grated Parmesan cheese, *DiGiorno*®

Here's what you do:

1 In large bowl, using a large spoon, combine popcorn and pretzel sticks.

2 Place butter in small microwave-safe bowl. Cover loosely with plastic wrap. Microwave on high setting (100% power) for 30 seconds or until melted. Using oven mitts, remove from microwave. Carefully remove plastic wrap. Drizzle butter over popcorn and pretzels.

3 Sprinkle mixture with Parmesan cheese. With clean hands, toss together to coat. Serve immediately or store in an airtight container for up to 3 days.

Popcorn Nachos

Start to Finish 15 minutes Makes 4 cups

Here's what you do:

1 Preheat oven to 350 degrees F. Line baking sheet with aluminum foil.

2 Spread popped corn on prepared baking sheet, removing any unpopped kernels. Sprinkle taco seasoning evenly over popcorn. Sprinkle with cheese.

3 Place baking sheet in preheated oven. Bake for 2 to 4 minutes or until cheese is melted. Using oven mitts, remove from oven.

4 Using a heat-resistant spatula, transfer nachos to a serving plate or bowl. Top with salsa to serve.

Tools you'll need:

* Measuring cups
* Measuring spoons
* Baking sheet
* Aluminum foil
* Oven mitts
* Heat-resistant spatula
* Serving plate or bowl

Food you'll need:

4   cups popped popcorn

1   teaspoon taco seasoning, *McCormick*®

$1\frac{1}{2}$ cups shredded Mexican cheese blend, *Kraft*®

$\frac{1}{4}$ cup mild salsa, *Pace*®

Triple Tostadas

Start to Finish 20 minutes Makes 12 tostadas

Tools you'll need:

* Measuring spoons
* Measuring cups
* Baking sheet
* Aluminum foil
* Spoon
* Microwave-safe bowl
* Plastic wrap
* Oven mitts
* Medium skillet
* Wooden spoon
* Heat-resistant spatula
* Serving plate

Food you'll need:

1/2 cup fat-free refried beans, *Rosarita*®

4 ounces ground beef or ground turkey

1 tablespoon taco seasoning, *McCormick*®

36 tortilla chip rounds, *Mission*®

3/4 cup shredded cheddar cheese, *Kraft*®

3/4 cup shredded lettuce

1/2 cup mild salsa, *Pace*®

1/4 cup sour cream, *Knudsen*®

Here's what you do:

1. Preheat oven to 350 degrees F. Line baking sheet with aluminum foil.

2. Spoon beans into microwave-safe bowl. Cover loosely with plastic wrap. Microwave on high setting (100% power) for 1 to 2 minutes, stirring once halfway through cooking time (be careful; beans will be hot!). Using oven mitts, remove from microwave. Carefully remove plastic wrap. Stir; set aside.

3. In a medium skillet, using a wooden spoon, stir together ground beef or turkey and taco seasoning. Place on burner; turn burner to medium-high. Cook and stir until meat is browned; remove from heat.

4. Top 1 tortilla chip round with 1 teaspoon beans and 1 teaspoon ground meat mixture. Top with another tortilla chip. Repeat bean and meat layers once more. Top with a third round. Sprinkle 1 tablespoon cheese on top of last round. Repeat to make 12 tostadas. Evenly arrange tostadas on prepared baking sheet.

5. Place baking sheet in oven. Bake for 2 to 4 minutes or until cheese is melted. Using oven mitts, remove from oven. Using a heat-resistant spatula, carefully transfer to a serving plate. Serve tostadas with shredded lettuce, salsa, and sour cream on the side.

Microwave Method: Prepare recipe as directed through step 4, except arrange assembled tostadas on a microwave-safe plate. Microwave tostadas, uncovered, on high setting (100% power) for 1 to 2 minutes or until cheese is melted. Serve as directed in step 5.

Pizza Dogs

Prep 20 minutes Bake 12 minutes Makes 10 frankfurters

Tools you'll need:

* Measuring cups
* Measuring spoons
* Baking sheet
* Aluminum foil
* Table knife
* Oven mitts
* Microwave-safe bowl
* Plastic wrap

Food you'll need:

1 can (11-ounce) refrigerated breadsticks, *Pillsbury®*

1½ cups roasted garlic-and-herb pasta sauce, *Prego®*

¼ cup grated Parmesan cheese, *DiGiorno®*

1 package (16-ounce) turkey frankfurters, *Oscar Mayer®* or *Louis Rich®*

¼ cup shredded mozzarella cheese, *Kraft®*

Here's what you do:

1 Preheat oven to 375 degrees F. Line a baking sheet with aluminum foil.

2 Unroll breadstick dough and separate into individual pieces. Place them vertically a few inches apart on prepared baking sheet.

3 Using a table knife, spread 1 teaspoon pasta sauce on the top of each breadstick. Sprinkle each with grated Parmesan cheese.

4 Place a frankfurter at one end of each breadstick so it makes the letter "L." Pinch dough around the end of the frankfurter. Wrap dough around frankfurter in a spiral completely covering the meat. Pinch dough together at the other end. Repeat with remaining breadsticks and frankfurters. Arrange wrapped frankfurters evenly on baking sheet.

5 Sprinkle wrapped frankfurters with mozzarella cheese. Place baking sheet in preheated oven. Bake for 12 to 15 minutes. Using oven mitts, remove from oven.

6 While pizza dogs are baking, place remaining pasta sauce in a microwave-safe bowl. Cover loosely with plastic wrap. Microwave on high setting (100% power) for 1 to 1½ minutes or until heated through. Using oven mitts, remove from microwave. Carefully remove plastic wrap. Serve pizza dogs with heated pasta sauce for dipping.

Stuffed Celery

Prep 10 minutes **Stand** 30 minutes **Makes** 12 pieces

Here's what you do:

1 Unwrap cream cheese and place in a medium bowl. Let stand at room temperature for 30 minutes to soften.

2 Wash celery and pat dry with paper towels. Have an adult use a sharp knife to cut off ends of celery and cut each rib in half crosswise.

3 Using a spoon, stir honey, nuts, and cranberries into softened cream cheese.

4 Using a table knife, spread 2 tablespoons cream cheese mixture onto each celery piece.

Tools you'll need:

* Measuring cups
* Measuring spoons
* Medium bowl
* Paper towels
* Sharp knife
* Cutting board
* Spoon
* Table knife

Food you'll need:

1   package (8-ounce) light cream cheese, *Philadelphia®*

6   ribs celery

1   cup honey, *SueBee®*

¼   cup chopped nut topping, *Planters®*

¼   cup dried cranberries, *Ocean Spray®*

Funtastic Fruit Leather

Prep 20 minutes Dry 6 hours Makes 12 strips

Tools you'll need:

* 17×12-inch rimmed baking sheet
* Plastic wrap
* Blender
* Rubber spatula
* Oven mitts
* Wire cooling rack
* Sharp knife
* Cutting board
* Airtight container

Food you'll need:

1 bag (16-ounce) desired loose-pack frozen fruit, thawed*

Sugar (optional)

Here's what you do:

1 Preheat oven to 140 degrees F or warm setting. Loosely line a 17×12-inch rimmed baking sheet with plastic wrap, leaving extra plastic wrap draping over edges; set aside.

2 Place thawed fruit in blender. Cover; turn on blender. Blend until fruit is pureed. If needed, add some sugar to taste. If necessary, turn off blender and scrape sides with a rubber spatula.

3 Pour puree onto prepared baking sheet. Tilt pan back and forth until there is a thin layer of fruit covering the bottom. Loosen plastic wrap from sides; fold edges over fruit.

4 Place baking pan in preheated oven. Leave oven door open about 4 to 6 inches to allow moisture to escape. Dry fruit about 6 hours or until middle of puree is barely sticky (have an adult check for doneness). (If the fruit does not dry enough, it will mold during storage.) Using oven mitts, remove from oven. Place on wire rack; cool completely.

5 To remove from pan, peel plastic wrap back. Working from one of the short ends, roll fruit leather up, peeling back the plastic wrap as you go.

6 Have an adult use a sharp knife to cut fruit leather into 1-inch-wide strips. Store in an airtight container at room temperature for up to 3 weeks. For longer storage, store in the refrigerator for 2 months or in the freezer for 3 months.

***Note:** If you choose fruits that brown, such as peaches, add 1 tablespoon of fresh lemon juice to fruit in the blender.

Tip: If fruit leather becomes too dry and brittle, crush it and sprinkle over cereal or yogurt or add it to cookie dough.

Triple Chocolate Ice Cream Sandwiches

Prep 10 minutes **Bake** 10 minutes per batch **Stand** 10 minutes
Freeze 1 hour 30 minutes **Makes** 8 sandwiches

Here's what you do:

1 Preheat oven to 375 degrees F. Place butter in a small bowl; let stand at room temperature to soften. In another small bowl, using a fork, beat egg lightly.

2 In a large bowl, using a wooden spoon, stir together cookie mix, miniature candy-coated chocolate pieces, the softened butter, and the beaten egg to form a dough. Drop dough by heaping teaspoons* 2 inches apart onto ungreased cookie sheets. Slightly flatten mounds.

3 Place 1 cookie sheet in preheated oven. Bake for 10 to 14 minutes. Using oven mitts, remove from oven. Place baking sheet on a wire rack; cool for 1 minute. Using a heat-resistant spatula, transfer cookies to a wire rack; cool completely. Repeat process with remaining cookie sheets. Place cooled cookies in a freezer container. Freeze for 1 hour.

4 For sandwiches, let ice cream soften at room temperature for 10 minutes. Remove cookies from freezer. Place a scoop of ice cream on the flat sides of 8 cookies. Top each with a second cookie, flat side down. Press cookies together until ice cream reaches cookie edges. Wrap each sandwich in plastic wrap. Freeze for 30 minutes.

***Note:** To drop dough on the cookie sheet, use a teaspoon from your parents' silverware drawer (the small spoon rather than the soup spoon). Do not use a teaspoon from your measuring spoons.

Tools you'll need:

* 2 small bowls
* Fork
* Large bowl
* Wooden spoon
* Teaspoon*
* Cookie sheets
* Oven mitts
* Wire cooling racks
* Heat-resistant spatula
* Freezer container
* Ice cream scoop
* Plastic wrap

Food you'll need:

1   stick ($\frac{1}{2}$ cup) butter

1   large egg

1   package (17.5-ounce) chocolate chip cookie mix, *Betty Crocker*®

$\frac{1}{2}$ cup miniature candy-coated milk chocolate pieces, *M&M's*®

2   pints chocolate chunk or chocolate chocolate chip ice cream, *Häagen-Dazs*®

Sleepover Sensations

It all started with my 13-year-old niece, Danielle. Danielle's my blonde bombshell and always blows my heart away. She loves lots of things—surfer girl movies, snowboarding, Halloween—but food wasn't one of them. At least not my food. When she was a little girl, Danielle would come to Aunt Sandy's for sleepover weekends and refuse to eat. I'd make pizza. She'd want tacos. I'd make quesadillas. She'd say, "Where are the pineapples?" So I took her to the store and let her pick out what she wanted. Soon we were making—and eating—Taco Pizza, Aloha Quesadillas, and other fab food like Fruit Wands and Cheesecake Sandwiches. Sleepovers became the greatest. Not to mention the food.

The Recipes

Taco Pizza

Prep 20 minutes Bake 8 minutes Makes 4 servings

Tools you'll need:

* Measuring cups
* Sharp knife
* Cutting board
* Strainer
* Small bowl
* Large skillet
* Wooden spoon
* Oven mitts
* Medium bowl
* Baking sheet
* Rubber spatula
* Slotted spoon
* Pizza cutter

Food you'll need:

¼	head lettuce
1	tomato
1	can (2.25-ounce) sliced black olives, *Early California*®
1	pound ground beef
1	packet (1.25-ounce) taco seasoning, *McCormick*®
1	10-ounce Italian bread shell, *Boboli*®
1	cup mild salsa, *Pace*®
1	cup shredded Mexican cheese blend, *Kraft*®

Here's what you do:

1. Preheat oven to 425 degrees F. Have an adult use a sharp knife to chop lettuce and dice tomato; set aside. Using a strainer set over small bowl, drain olives; discard liquid. Place olives in bowl; set aside.

2. In a large skillet, stir together ground beef and taco seasoning. Place on burner; turn burner to medium-high. Cook and stir mixture with a wooden spoon for about 10 minutes or until ground beef is brown. Remove from heat. Have an adult help you drain mixture through strainer. Place in a medium bowl; cool.

3. Place bread shell on a baking sheet. Using a rubber spatula, evenly spread salsa over shell. Sprinkle cheese evenly on top. Using a slotted spoon, top with browned meat.

4. Place baking sheet in preheated oven. Bake for 8 to 10 minutes or until cheese is melted. Using oven mitts, remove pizza from oven.

5. Top taco pizza with chopped lettuce, diced tomato, and sliced olives. Have an adult use a pizza cutter to cut pizza into wedges. Serve hot.

Potato Bombs

Start to Finish 25 minutes Makes 4 servings

Here's what you do:

1. Have an adult use a sharp knife to chop about ¼ cup chives; Place in a small bowl; set aside.

2. Place 2 potatoes on a microwave-safe plate. Place in microwave. Cook on high setting (100% power) for 10 to 14 minutes or until tender. Using oven mitts, carefully remove from microwave. (Potatoes will be HOT!) Repeat with remaining potatoes. Cool potatoes for 5 minutes or until cool enough to handle. Remove plastic from potatoes.

3. Using a table knife, cut a slit lengthwise into the top of each potato. Spread the top of the potato apart about 2 inches. With a fork, break up the insides of the potato. Top each potato with 2 tablespoons chili and 1 tablespoon shredded cheese.

4. Place 2 potatoes on a microwave-safe plate. Return to microwave. Cook on high setting (100% power) for 2 minutes. Using oven mitts, remove potatoes from the microwave. Repeat with remaining potatoes.

5. Using a heat-resistant spatula, transfer each potato to a dinner plate. Top with 1 tablespoon sour cream and 1 tablespoon chives.

*Note: If you like, replace chives with real bacon pieces, *Hormel*®.

**Note: Potatoes for the microwave are wrapped in plastic and found in the produce section of the supermarket.

Other Topping Ideas: Another time, try topping plain potatoes with marinara sauce, shredded mozzarella cheese, and diced pepperoni. Or top plain potatoes with shredded cheddar cheese and broccoli florets.

Tools you'll need:

* Measuring cups
* Sharp knife
* Cutting board
* 2 microwave-safe plates
* Oven mitts
* Table knife
* Fork
* Measuring spoons
* Heat-resistant spatula
* 4 dinner plates

Food you'll need:

Chives or scallions (green onions)*

4 potatoes for the microwave, *Melissa's*® Micro Baker Potatoes**

1 cup chili con carne, *Dennison's*®

¼ cup shredded cheddar cheese, *Kraft*®

¼ cup sour cream, *Knudsen*®

BBQ Chicken Pizza

Start to Finish 25 minutes Makes 4 servings

Tools you'll need:

* Baking sheet
* Sharp knife
* Cutting board
* Oven mitts
* Spoon
* Pizza cutter

Food you'll need:

Olive oil cooking spray, *Mazola® Pure*

1 cup diced green apple

1 can (13.8-ounce) refrigerated pizza dough, *Pillsbury®*

1 cup barbecue sauce, *Bull's-Eye®*

2 cups shredded mozzarella cheese, *Kraft®*

1 package (6-ounce) fully cooked grilled chicken strips, *Foster Farms®*

1/4 cup real bacon bits, *Hormel®*

Here's what you do:

Preheat oven to 425°F. Lightly spray baking sheet with cooking spray. Have an adult use a sharp knife to chop enough green apple to make 1 cup.

Carefully remove pizza dough from can. Unroll dough and place on prepared baking sheet. Press out dough to form a 13×9-inch rectangle. Place baking sheet in preheated oven. Bake for 7 minutes or until crust is just beginning to brown. Using oven mitts, remove crust from oven.

With a spoon, spread barbecue sauce over pizza, leaving a 1-inch border. Top pizza with chopped apple, mozzarella cheese, chicken strips, and bacon pieces. Return crust to oven. Bake for 8 to 10 minutes or until crust is golden brown and cheese is melted and bubbly. Using oven mitts, remove pizza from oven. Have an adult use a pizza cutter to cut pizza into squares. Serve warm.

Aloha Quesadillas

Start to Finish 30 minutes Makes 4 quesadillas

Here's what you do:

Using a strainer set over small bowl, drain pineapple. Discard liquid; set pineapple aside. On a cutting board, top 1 tortilla with 3 slices of Canadian bacon, one-fourth of the pineapple, and $\frac{1}{2}$ cup of the cheese. Top with another tortilla. Repeat to make a total of 4 quesadillas.

Spray a large nonstick skillet with cooking spray. Place on burner; turn burner to medium-high. Carefully slide 1 quesadilla into skillet. Cook for 3 minutes. Have an adult use a heat-resistant spatula to carefully flip quesadilla. Cook for 3 minutes more. Remove skillet from heat. Using the spatula, transfer quesadilla to a serving plate. Using a table knife, cut into quarters. Repeat with remaining quesadillas. Serve warm.

Microwave Directions: Assemble quesadillas as directed in step 1. Place each quesadilla on a microwave-safe plate. Place 1 quesadilla in the microwave. Cook on high setting (100% power) for 2 to 3 minutes. Using oven mitts, remove from microwave. Using a table knife, cut into quarters. Repeat with remaining quesadillas.

Tools you'll need:

* Measuring cups
* Strainer
* Small bowl
* Cutting board
* Large nonstick skillet
* Heat-resistant spatula
* Oven mitts
* Serving plate
* Table knife

Food you'll need:

1   can (8-ounce) pineapple chunks, *Dole®*

8   taco-size (8-inch) flour tortillas, *Mission®*

1   package (5-ounce) Canadian bacon slices

2   cups shredded Monterey Jack cheese, *Kraft®*

Canola oil cooking spray, *Mazola® Pure*

Fondue Party!

Start to Finish 20 minutes Makes 6 servings

Tools you'll need:

* Measuring cups
* Measuring spoons
* Table knife
* 2 microwave-safe bowls
* Oven mitts
* 2 wooden spoons
* Oven mitts
* Paper towels

Food you'll need:

FOR CHEESE FONDUE

1   package (8-ounce) cream cheese, *Philadelphia*®

1   can (10-ounce) condensed cheddar cheese soup, *Campbell's*®

½   cup half-and-half

½   cup shredded cheddar cheese, *Kraft*®

Cut-up vegetables* and pretzel sticks

FOR CHOCOLATE FONDUE

12 ounces semisweet chocolate pieces, *Nestlé*®

1   cup half-and-half

1   teaspoon ground cinnamon, *McCormick*®

Assorted dippers (such as marshmallows, strawberries, bananas, and/or graham cracker sticks)

Here's what you do:

For Cheese Fondue, using a table knife, cut cream cheese into 1-inch pieces. Place in a microwave-safe bowl. Cover bowl with a paper towel. Microwave on medium-high setting (80% power) for 1½ minutes. Using oven mitts, remove from microwave. Remove paper towel. Using a wooden spoon, stir in cheddar cheese soup, the ½ cup half-and-half, and the cheddar cheese. Replace paper towel. Return to microwave. Cook on medium-high setting (80% power) about 5 minutes or until smooth, stirring every minute. Serve with cut-up vegetables and pretzel sticks.

***Note:** Have an adult help you cut up your favorite fresh vegetables, such as celery sticks and sweet peppers.

For Chocolate Fondue, in another microwave-safe bowl, combine chocolate pieces, the 1 cup half-and-half, and the cinnamon. Cover bowl with a paper towel. Microwave on medium-high setting (80% power) for 1½ minutes. Using oven mitts, remove from microwave. Remove paper towel. With another wooden spoon, stir chocolate mixture for 1 minute. Replace paper towel. Return to microwave. Cook for 1 minute more. Using oven mitts, remove from microwave. With wooden spoon, stir until chocolate is melted completely. Serve with assorted dippers.

Fruit Wands

Tools you'll need:

* Measuring cups
* Measuring spoons
* Small bowl
* Whisk
* Sharp knife
* Cutting board
* Table knife
* Eight 8-inch wooden skewers
* Spoon
* Serving plates

Food you'll need:

FOR DIPPING SAUCE

2 cups fat-free vanilla yogurt, *Dannon*®

2 tablespoons honey, *SueBee*®

FOR FRUIT WANDS:

1 apple

2 bananas

1 container (2-pound) precut mixed fruit (such as pineapple, cantaloupe, melon, watermelon), *Ready Pac*®

1 cantaloupe

Here's what you do:

For Dipping Sauce, in a bowl, combine yogurt and honey with a whisk; set aside.

For Fruit Wands, have an adult use a sharp knife to core apple and cut into bite-size pieces. With a table knife, cut banana into bite-size chunks. To make wands, slide chunks of fruit onto eight 8-inch skewers, leaving 1 inch at both ends of each skewer.

Have an adult use a sharp knife to cut the cantaloupe in half. Remove all seeds from the insides of both halves with a spoon. Place one half of cantaloupe upside down on a serving plate. Stick the pointy ends of the skewers into the cantaloupe, spacing them evenly.

Pour Dipping Sauce into the other cantaloupe half (which serves as a bowl). Place cantaloupe bowl on the serving plate. To eat, dip the Fruit Wands in the Dipping Sauce.

Cheesecake Sandwiches

Start to Finish 10 minutes Makes 8 sandwiches

Here's what you do:

Set out 8 graham cracker squares. Use a table knife to spread each of the 8 squares with 1 tablespoon cream cheese. Top the cream cheese on each square with 1 tablespoon strawberry preserves; spread with table knife. Top each square with 1 of the remaining cracker squares; press together.

Tools you'll need:

* Measuring cups
* Table knife

Food you'll need:

16 2-cracker squares of graham crackers, *Honey Maid*®

½ cup strawberry-flavor cream cheese, *Kraft*®

½ cup strawberry preserves, *Smucker's*®

Groovy Goodies

At age 9, my niece, Stephanie, is the little hostess with the mostest. Plan a party and she'll work up the menu, organize the ingredients, and make the table look amazing. But what she's really into is baking. She'll join me on my Food Network® show and we'll bake up goodies by the gazillion. Fiendin' for fun food? Cherry Cream Cheese Blondies and Peanut Butter Cup Cupcakes are all that. Mo-om, turn the oven on. NOT! No-Bake Oreo® Cheesecake and Banana Split Mini Pies need just two hands and a spoon. For the next bake sale, let the others bring some half-baked brownies—you're bringing the good stuff.

The Recipes

Rainbow Ribbon Cake

Prep 40 minutes Bake 32 minutes Cool 10 minutes
Chill 3 hours Makes 1 cake (10 servings)

Tools you'll need:

* Measuring cups and spoons
* Two 8-inch round cake pans
* Large bowl
* Handheld electric mixer
* Rubber spatula
* Oven mitts
* Wire cooling racks
* 1 table knife
* 6 small bowls
* Medium saucepan
* 6 spoons and 1 fork
* Plastic wrap
* Serving plate
* Icing spatula or table knife

Food you'll need:

FOR CAKE

Butter-flavor cooking spray, *Mazola® Pure*

1 box (18.25-ounce) white cake mix, *Betty Crocker®*

1¼ cups water

⅓ cup canola oil, *Wesson®*

3 large egg whites

½ teaspoon vanilla, *McCormick®*

1 tablespoon each lemon-, orange-, cherry-, grape-, lime-, and blue raspberry-flavor gelatin, *Jell-O®*

2 cups water

Here's what you do:

Preheat oven to 350 degrees F. Lightly spray two 8-inch round cake pans with cooking spray; set aside. In a large bowl, place cake mix, the 1¼ cups water, the canola oil, egg whites, and vanilla. Using an electric mixer, beat mixture on low speed for 30 seconds. Using a rubber spatula, scrape down sides of bowl; beat on medium speed for 2 minutes. Divide mixture evenly between cake pans.

Place cake pans in preheated oven. Bake for 32 to 36 minutes or until a toothpick inserted into the centers of cakes comes out clean. Using oven mitts, remove from oven. Place on wire racks; cool for 10 to 15 minutes. Using a table knife, loosen edges of each cake layer. Place a wire rack on top of each cake layer; invert. Remove cake pan. Place a second wire rack on top of cake; invert. Remove top wire rack. Cool completely. Wash cake pans; dry.

Place cooled cake layers back into cake pans; set aside. Place 1 tablespoon of each gelatin flavor in a separate bowl. Fill a saucepan with 2 cups water. Place on burner; bring to a boil over high heat. Have an adult divide hot water into ⅓-cup portions. Stir ⅓ cup boiling water into each bowl of gelatin; stir with separate spoons until dissolved.

Using a fork, prick holes 2 inches apart around border of 1 cake layer. Carefully spoon 1 flavor of gelatin into holes. Prick another ring of holes inside the first ring. Spoon a different flavor of gelatin into the holes. Prick holes for the center ring. Spoon a third flavor of gelatin into the holes. Repeat with remaining cake and gelatin. Cover cakes with plastic wrap. Place in the refrigerator for 3 to 4 hours.

5 Remove cake layers from refrigerator. Fill the kitchen sink with about 1 inch of warm water. To remove cakes from pans, dip the bottoms of cake pans into warm water (keep the water out of the cake pans!). Run a table knife around the edge to loosen cake layer. Place cake layers upright on wire racks by doing the same thing you did in step 2.

6 Place 1 cake layer on a serving plate. Using an icing spatula or table knife, spread whipped frosting evenly on top. Add second cake layer and frost top and sides of entire cake. Using the colored decorating icings, create rainbow ribbons on the cake sides. Decorate with Lifesavers®, birthday candles, and candy sprinkles (optional).

Food you'll need:

FOR DECORATING

2 cans (12 ounces each) whipped fluffy white frosting, *Betty Crocker®*

Various colors of decorating icing, *Cake Mate®*

Lifesavers®, birthday candles, and candy sprinkles (optional)

Tie-Dyed Cupcakes

Prep 10 minutes **Bake** 21 minutes **Cool** 30 minutes **Makes** 24 cupcakes

Tools you'll need:

* Measuring cups
* 2 muffin pans with twelve 2½-inch cups each
* Cupcake liners
* Large mixing bowl
* Handheld electric mixer
* Rubber spatula
* Ladle
* Oven mitts
* Wooden toothpicks
* Wire cooling racks
* Icing spatula or table knife
* Serving platter

Food you'll need:

1 box (18.25-ounce) white cake mix, *Betty Crocker*®

1¼ cups white grape juice, *Ocean Spray*®

⅓ cup canola oil, *Wesson*®

1 bottle (1.25-ounce) colored snowflake sprinkles, *Cake Mate*®

1 bottle (1.85-ounce) rainbow sprinkles, *Cake Mate*®

1 can (12-ounce) whipped fluffy white frosting, *Betty Crocker*®

Assorted colors of decorating gels, *Cake Mate*®

Here's what you do:

Preheat oven to 350 degrees F. Line all the 2½-inch muffin cups (24 total) with cupcake liners; set aside.

In a large bowl, place cake mix, grape juice, and oil. Using an electric mixer, beat on medium speed for 1 minute. Using a rubber spatula, scrape down the sides of the bowl; add both bottles of sprinkles. Beat for 30 seconds. Using a ladle, carefully fill each lined muffin cup two-thirds full.

Place muffin pans in preheated oven. Bake for 21 for 26 minutes or until a toothpick inserted into the center of a cupcake comes out clean (with no batter stuck to it).

Using oven mitts, remove from oven. Place pans on wire racks; let stand about 30 minutes or until completely cool.

Using an icing spatula or table knife, spread 2 tablespoons fluffy white frosting on each cupcake. Using assorted colors of decorating gels, start in the middle of each cupcake and make circles outward to the edge. Using a toothpick, begin at the edge of the cupcake and drag the tip of toothpick to the center of the cupcake to make a spider web effect. Repeat this step around each cupcake, turning the cupcakes as you go. Place cupcakes on a serving platter.

Peanut Butter Cup Cupcakes

Prep 10 minutes **Bake** 21 minutes **Cool** 30 minutes (cupcakes)
Chill 30 minutes (cupcake filling) **Makes** 24 cupcakes

Here's what you do:

1 Preheat oven to 350 degrees F. Line all the 2½-inch muffin cups (24 total) with cupcake liners; set aside.

2 In a large mixing bowl, place cake mix, chocolate milk, oil, and eggs. Using an electric mixer, beat on low speed for 30 seconds. Scrape down the sides of the bowl with a rubber spatula; beat on medium speed for 1 minute.

3 Using a ladle, carefully fill each lined muffin cup two-thirds full. Place muffin pans in preheated oven. Bake for 21 to 26 minutes or until a toothpick inserted in the center of a cupcake comes out clean (with no batter stuck to it).

4 Using oven mitts, remove from oven. Place on wire racks; let stand about 30 minutes or until completely cool.

5 Meanwhile, for filling, in another large mixing bowl, combine pudding mix, milk, and peanut butter. Using a whisk, beat for 2 minutes until smooth and thickened. Place in refrigerator; chill for 30 minutes.

6 Spoon filling into a pastry bag fitted with a medium round tip. Fill cupcakes by inserting tip into the top of each cupcake and squeezing about 2 tablespoons of filling into each. Using an icing spatula or table knife, spread 2 tablespoons frosting on each cupcake top.

Tools you'll need:

* Measuring cups
* 2 muffin pans with twelve 2½-inch cups each
* Cupcake liners
* 2 large mixing bowls
* Handheld electric mixer
* Rubber spatula and a ladle
* Oven mitts
* Wooden toothpicks
* Wire cooling racks
* Whisk and spoon
* Pastry bag and medium round decorating tip
* Icing spatula or table knife

Food you'll need:

1   box (18.25-ounce) dark chocolate cake mix, *Betty Crocker®*

1⅓ cups chocolate milk

½   cup canola oil, *Wesson®*

3   large eggs

1¼ cups milk

1   box (3.4-ounce) butterscotch instant pudding and pie filling mix, *Jell-O®*

½   cup creamy peanut butter, *Skippy®*

1   can (12-ounce) dark chocolate frosting, *Betty Crocker®*

Crazy Cranberry Can Cakes

Prep 20 minutes Bake 25 minutes Makes 5 cakes

Tools you'll need:

* Measuring cups and spoons
* Strainer and small bowl
* Five 16-ounce cranberry cans or similar size cans
* Large bowl
* Wooden spoon
* Baking sheet
* Oven mitts
* Wooden toothpicks
* Wire cooling rack
* Table knife
* Plastic wrap
* Medium skillet

Food you'll need:

2   cans (16 ounces each) whole cranberries, *Ocean Spray®*

    Butter-flavor cooking spray, *Mazola® Pure*

2   boxes (17.5 ounces each) blueberry muffin mix, *Krusteaz®*

2½ cups shredded coconut, toasted,* *Baker's®*

2   cups white cranberry juice, *Ocean Spray®*

2   teaspoons vanilla extract, *McCormick®*

2   teaspoons ground cinnamon, *McCormick®*

Here's what you do:

1 Preheat oven to 400 degrees F. Place cranberries in a strainer; rinse under cold running water. Place in a small bowl. Spray the insides of five 16-ounce cans with cooking spray. (Only use cans that are free from dents. Throw away the cans after using.) Set prepared cans aside.

2 In a large bowl, stir together drained cranberries, muffin mix, coconut, cranberry juice, vanilla, and cinnamon with a wooden spoon. Divide mixture among the prepared cans; place cans on a baking sheet.

3 Place baking sheet in preheated oven. Bake for 30 to 35 minutes or until a toothpick inserted in the center of a cake comes out clean. Using oven mitts, remove from oven. Place cans on a wire rack. Cool completely.

4 Loosen edges of cakes by running a table knife between cakes and edges of cans. Remove cakes by inverting cans. Wrap cakes in plastic wrap. If you like, decorate cakes with colored paper and ribbon to take to a bake sale.

*Toasted coconut: Place coconut in a dry skillet. Place on a burner; turn burner to medium-low. Using a wooden spoon, cook and stir until golden brown. Remove from burner; cool completely.

No-Bake Oreo® Cheesecake

Tools you'll need:

* Measuring cups
* Measuring spoons
* Large zip-top plastic bag
* Rolling pin
* Microwave-safe bowl
* Oven mitts
* Large mixing bowl
* Electric mixer
* Rubber spatula
* Sharp knife

Food you'll need:

Chocolate sandwich cookies with white filling, *Oreo*®

1　package (8-ounce) cream cheese, *Philadelphia*®

½　cup sugar

1　cup sour cream, *Knudsen*®

1　teaspoon vanilla, *McCormick*®

1　container (8-ounce) frozen whipped topping, thawed, *Cool Whip*®

1　9-inch premade chocolate-flavor piecrust, *Keebler*®

10　chocolate sandwich cookies with white filling, *Oreo*®

Here's what you do:

1 Place several whole chocolate sandwich cookies in a large zip-top plastic bag. Using a rolling pin, crush cookies into small pieces. Measure out 1½ cups; set aside.

2 Place cream cheese in a microwave-safe bowl. Place in microwave. Cook on medium-high setting (80% power) for 1 minute or until softened. Using oven mitts, remove from microwave.

3 In a large mixing bowl, place softened cream cheese and sugar. Using an electric mixer, beat on low speed until creamy. Add sour cream and vanilla; beat until well combined. Using a rubber spatula, stir in whipped topping and crushed chocolate cookies.

4 Spread mixture evenly into piecrust. Place in the refrigerator; chill for 4 to 5 hours before serving. Have an adult use a sharp knife to cut pie into 10 slices. Top each slice with a whole chocolate sandwich cookie.

Banana Split Mini Pies

Start to Finish 15 minutes Makes 6 mini pies

Here's what you do:

Using a table knife, chop banana into small pieces. Spoon 1 tablespoon of vanilla pudding into each of the 6 tart shells. Top each with about 1 tablespoon chopped banana and 2 tablespoons chocolate pudding. Add 1 teaspoon of strawberry preserves to each mini pie.

Top each mini pie with whipped cream. Sprinkle with about $\frac{1}{4}$ teaspoon nut topping. Top each mini pie with a cherry.

Tools you'll need:

* Measuring spoons
* Table knife
* Spoon

Food you'll need:

1   small banana

6   tablespoons prepared vanilla pudding, *Kraft® Handi Snacks*

1   package graham cracker tart shells, *Keebler®* (6 shells)

$\frac{3}{4}$ cup prepared chocolate fudge pudding, *Kraft® Handi Snacks*

Strawberry preserves, *Smucker's®*

Pressurized whipped cream, *Reddi Whip®*

$1\frac{1}{2}$ teaspoons nut topping, *Planters®*

6   maraschino cherries

PB&J Bread Pudding

Prep 15 minutes **Chill** 1 hour **Bake** 1 hour **Makes** 8 servings

Tools you'll need:

* Measuring cups
* Measuring spoons
* 2½-quart casserole
* Baking sheet
* Aluminum foil
* Table knife
* Medium bowl
* Whisk
* Oven mitts
* Wire cooling rack
* Large spoon
* Dessert dishes

Food you'll need:

Butter-flavor cooking spray, *Mazola® Pure*

10 slices white bread, *Sara Lee®*

½ cup creamy peanut butter, *Skippy®*

½ cup strawberry preserves, *Smucker's®*

2 cups milk

3 large eggs

½ cup sugar

2 teaspoons vanilla, *McCormick®*

Here's what you do:

1. Preheat oven to 350 degrees F. Lightly spray a 2½-quart casserole with cooking spray; set aside. Line a baking sheet with aluminum foil; set aside.

2. To make peanut butter and jelly sandwiches, using a table knife, spread half of the bread slices with peanut butter. Spread strawberry preserves over the peanut butter. Top with remaining bread slices. Cut each sandwich into quarters diagonally to make 4 small triangles. Arrange sandwich triangles with points sticking up in prepared casserole. Set aside.

3. In a medium bowl, using a whisk, thoroughly combine milk, eggs, sugar, and vanilla. Pour over sandwiches. Place in the refrigerator; chill for 1 hour to let egg mixture soak into sandwiches.

4. Place baking dish on prepared baking sheet. Place baking sheet in preheated oven. Bake for 1 hour. Using oven mitts, remove from oven. Place on a wire rack; cool slightly.

5. Using a large spoon, divide bread pudding among dessert dishes. Serve warm.

Purple Strawberry Crumble

Prep 20 minutes **Bake** 55 minutes **Cool** 6 minutes **Makes** 8 servings

Here's what you do:

1 Preheat oven to 375 degrees F. Lightly spray a 2½-quart baking dish with cooking spray; set aside. Line a baking sheet with aluminum foil; set aside.

2 For filling, in a large bowl, place frozen fruit, granulated sugar, and cornstarch. Using a large spoon, stir together until fruit is coated and there is no white remaining from cornstarch. Spoon into prepared baking dish.

3 For topping, place butter in a microwave-safe bowl. Cover loosely with plastic wrap. Place in microwave. Cook on high setting (100% power) about 1 minute or until melted. Using oven mitts, remove from microwave. Carefully remove plastic wrap.

4 In medium bowl, using a spoon, stir together contents of oatmeal packets, baking mix, brown sugar, and melted butter. Stir until mixture is combined and crumbly. Sprinkle mixture evenly over fruit.

5 Place prepared baking dish on a foil-lined baking sheet. Place baking sheet in preheated oven. Bake for 55 to 60 minutes or until top is golden brown and fruit is bubbling.

6 Using oven mitts, remove from oven. Place on a wire rack; cool for 6 to 8 minutes. Using a large spoon, divide among dessert dishes. Serve warm.

Tools you'll need:

* Measuring cups and spoons
* 2½-quart baking dish
* Baking sheet
* Aluminum foil
* Large bowl
* 2 large spoons
* Microwave-safe bowl
* Plastic wrap
* Oven mitts
* Medium bowl
* Spoon
* Baking sheet
* Wire cooling rack
* Dessert dishes

Food you'll need:

Butter-flavor cooking spray, *Mazola® Pure*

1 package (16-ounce) frozen loose-pack whole unsweetened strawberries, *Dole®*

1 package (12-ounce) frozen loose-pack blueberries, *Dole®*

½ cup granulated sugar

2 tablespoons cornstarch

½ stick (¼ cup) butter

2 packets (35 grams each) blueberries and cream instant oatmeal, *Quaker®*

½ cup baking mix, *Bisquick®*

½ cup packed brown sugar, *C&H®*

Cherry Cream Cheese Blondies

Prep 20 minutes Bake 40 minutes Cool 15 minutes Makes 24 squares

Tools you'll need:

* Measuring cups
* Small bowl
* 13×9-inch baking pan
* Microwave-safe bowl
* Plastic wrap
* Oven mitts
* Large mixing bowl
* Handheld electric mixer
* Rubber spatula
* Tablespoon
* Spoon
* Wooden toothpicks
* Wire cooling rack
* Table knife

Food you'll need:

2 packages (8 ounces each) cream cheese, *Philadelphia*®

Butter-flavor cooking spray, *Mazola*® *Pure*

1 stick ($\frac{1}{2}$ cup) butter

1 box (18.25-ounce) yellow cake mix, *Betty Crocker*®

1 large egg

$\frac{1}{2}$ cup sugar

2 large eggs

1 can (20-ounce) light cherry pie filling or topping, *Comstock*® *More Fruit*

Here's what you do:

Place cream cheese in a small bowl. Let stand at room temperature for 30 minutes to soften. Spray a 13×9-inch baking pan with cooking spray; set aside.

Preheat oven to 350 degrees F. Place butter in a microwave-safe bowl. Cover loosely with plastic wrap. Place in microwave. Cook on high setting (100% power) for 1 minute or until melted. Using oven mitts, remove bowl from microwave. Carefully remove plastic wrap.

For the cake layer, in a large bowl, place cake mix, the 1 egg, and the melted butter. Using an electric mixer, beat mixture until well combined. With your hands, press mixture evenly onto bottom of prepared baking dish. Wash bowl and beaters; dry.

For the cream cheese layer, in the same clean bowl, place the softened cream cheese and sugar. Using an electric mixer, beat at low speed about 2 minutes or until mixture is creamy. Add the 2 eggs; beat on medium speed until mixture is combined.

Pour cream cheese mixture over cake mixture. With a rubber spatula, evenly spread in pan. Using a spoon, drop cherry pie filling evenly over cream cheese mixture.

Using oven mitts, place baking pan in preheated oven. Bake for 40 to 45 minutes or until a toothpick inserted into the center of the blondies (but not through cherries) comes out clean. Using oven mitts, remove baking pan from oven. Place on a wire rack; cool for 15 to 20 minutes. Using a table knife, cut into squares.

Cherry Chip Cookies

Prep 15 minutes Bake 10 minutes per batch Makes 26 cookies

Here's what you do:

Preheat oven to 350 degrees F. In a medium bowl, place sugar cookie dough, dried cherries, chocolate pieces, nut topping, and cherry extract. With your hands, knead mixture until thoroughly combined.

Drop by rounded teaspoonfuls* onto an ungreased cookie sheet. Using the palm of your hand, flatten cookies to $\frac{1}{4}$ inch thick.

Place cookie sheet in preheated oven. Bake for 10 to 12 minutes or until the edges are just golden brown. The middle should still be a little soft. (DO NOT overbake.)

Using oven mitts, remove from oven. Place cookie sheet on a wire rack; let cookies cool for 1 minute. Using a heat-resistant spatula, transfer cookies to a wire rack. Cool completely.

*Note: To drop dough on the cookie sheet, use a teaspoon from your parents' silverware drawer (the small spoon rather than the soup spoon). Do not use a teaspoon from your measuring spoons.

Tools you'll need:

* Measuring cups
* Measuring spoons
* Medium bowl
* Teaspoon*
* Cookie sheet
* Oven mitts
* Wire cooling rack
* Heat-resistant spatula

Food you'll need:

1   tube (18-ounce) refrigerated sugar cookie dough, *Pillsbury*®

$\frac{1}{2}$ cup dried cherries, *Mariani*®

$\frac{1}{3}$ cup white chocolate pieces, *Nestlé*®

$\frac{1}{4}$ cup chopped nut topping, *Planters*®

$\frac{1}{2}$ teaspoon cherry extract, *McCormick*®

Dino Cookies

Prep 25 minutes **Chill** 15 minutes **Bake** 10 minutes per batch **Makes** 28 cookies

Tools you'll need:

* Measuring cups
* Large bowl
* Wooden spoon
* Microwave-safe bowl
* Oven mitts
* Rolling pin
* 3-inch dinosaur-shape cookie cutter
* Heat-resistant spatula
* Cookie sheet
* Wire cooling racks

Food you'll need:

1   bag (17-ounce) sugar cookie mix, *Betty Crocker*®

¼   cup all-purpose flour

1   package (3-ounce) cream cheese, *Philadelphia*®

1   large egg

    All-purpose flour

1   bag (12-ounce) miniature candy-coated milk chocolate pieces, *M&M's*®

    Edible rock candy (optional)

    Edible Palm Trees (optional)

Here's what you do:

1 Preheat oven to 350 degrees F. In a large bowl, using a wooden spoon, stir together sugar cookie mix and flour.

2 Place cream cheese in a microwave-safe bowl. Place in microwave. Cook on medium-high setting (80% power) for 1 minute. Remove cream cheese from microwave. Add cream cheese and egg to cookie mix mixture. With a wooden spoon, stir until dough is well combined and forms a ball. Divide dough in half. Lightly sprinkle a flat rolling surface and a rolling pin with flour. Using the rolling pin, roll out half of the dough on the floured surface until $\frac{1}{4}$ inch thick, turning the dough so it does not stick.

3 Dip a 3-inch dinosaur-shape cookie cutter into flour. Cut out shapes at the center of the dough and work your way toward the edge, cutting shapes as close together as possible. Dip cookie cutter into flour as needed to prevent sticking. Using a spatula, place shapes on ungreased cookie sheet. Repeat with remaining dough. Decorate each cookie by pressing mini chocolate pieces into shapes. Place cookies in the refrigerator; chill for 15 minutes.

4 Place cookie sheet in oven. Bake for 10 to 12 minutes. Using oven mitts, remove from oven. Cool for 1 minute. Using the spatula, transfer cookies to wire racks; cool. Surround cookies with rock candy and Edible Palm Trees (optional).

Edible Palm Trees: On a surface lightly sprinkled with sugar, roll a large green gumdrop into a flat round piece. With a small knife, have an adult cut wedges from edges to resemble palm tree leaves. Form the gumdrop over a

Dynamite Drinks

Goblet of fire, shmire. A goblet of cool is so much … well, cooler. Or so say Taner, Rachel, Josh, Jacob, Cara, Mariah, Michaela, Christian, Aria, Talia, Jack, Amanda, Kyle, Hanna, Max, and Kaitlyn—the coolest kids I know. Tropical Cooler, Mango Tango, or Watermelon Spritzy, this chapter lets the whole gang sip their snacks morning, noon, and night. A Minty Chip Frappé is fit for an ice princess, while a Blue Lagoon will make any guy one chill dude. Sour Grapes? Absolutely! And an Orange Fizzy too. Pour on the charm with Fruity Lemonade—zowie, it's like love at first sight. Hey, choice is good. So break out the beverages, chill, and blend on. Cheers!

The Recipes

Orange Fizzy

Tools you'll need:

* Measuring cups
* Measuring spoons
* Sharp knife
* Cutting board
* Blender
* 4 large glasses
* Rubber spatula
* 4 drinking straws

Food you'll need:

1 orange (optional)
2 cups orange juice, *Tropicana*®
½ cup milk
8 ice cubes
2 tablespoons powdered sugar, *C&H*®

Here's what you do:

1 Have an adult use a sharp knife to slice orange (optional); set aside.

2 In a blender, place orange juice, milk, ice cubes, and powdered sugar. Cover; turn on blender. Blend for 1 to 2 minutes or until mixture is smooth and frothy. Pour into 4 large glasses; scrape blender sides with a rubber spatula.

3 Add a straw to each glass. Garnish glasses with an orange slice (optional).

Sour Grapes

Start to Finish 5 minutes Makes 2 (8-ounce) servings

Here's what you do:

1 In a pitcher, using a large spoon, stir together grape juice, drink mix, and lemon-line carbonated beverage.

2 Place ice cubes in 2 large glasses. Pour grape juice mixture evenly into each glass. Add a straw to each glass.

Tools you'll need:

* Measuring cups
* Pitcher
* Large spoon
* 2 large glasses
* 2 drinking straws

Food you'll need:

1 cup grape juice, chilled, *Welch's*®

½ cup nonalcoholic sweet-and-sour drink mix

½ cup lemon-lime carbonated beverage, chilled, *Sprite*®

Ice cubes

Watermelon Spritzy

Start to Finish 10 minutes Makes 2 (8-ounce) servings

Tools you'll need:

* Measuring cups
* Measuring spoons
* Sharp knife
* Cutting board
* Blender
* Rubber spatula
* Strainer
* Pitcher
* 2 large glasses
* 2 drinking straws

Food you'll need:

Watermelon

1 cup lemon-lime carbonated beverage, chilled, *Sprite*®

1 tablespoon grenadine, *Rose's*®

Ice cubes

Melon Skewers (optional)

Here's what you do:

1 Have an adult use a sharp knife to chop enough watermelon to make 1 cup (remove seeds before measuring). In a blender, place watermelon, lemon-lime carbonated beverage, and grenadine. Cover; turn on blender. Blend for 20 to 30 seconds or until slushy. Use a rubber spatula to scrape sides of blender.

2 Pour mixture through a strainer into a pitcher. Fill two large glasses with ice cubes. Pour watermelon mixture over ice. Add a straw to each glass. Garnish with Melon Skewers (optional).

Melon Skewers: To make skewers, use a melon baller to scoop 2 balls each from a watermelon, cantaloupe, and honeydew melon. Thread 1 of each type of melon ball onto a wooden skewer.

Fruity Lemonade

Start to Finish 5 minutes Makes 6 (8-ounce) servings

Here's what you do:

Have an adult use a sharp knife to slice lemon; set aside. In a large pitcher, using a large spoon, stir together water, lemonade concentrate, sugar, gelatin, and drink mix.

Place ice cubes in 6 large glasses. Pour lemonade mixture into each glass. Add straws to glasses. Garnish each glass with a lemon slice.

1

2

Tools you'll need:

* Measuring cups
* Measuring spoons
* Sharp knife
* Cutting board
* Large pitcher
* Large spoon
* 6 large glasses
* 6 drinking straws

Food you'll need:

1   lemon

6   cups cold water

6   tablespoons frozen lemonade concentrate, thawed, *Minute Maid®*

¼   cup sugar

1   teaspoon sugar-free peach-flavor gelatin, *Jell-O®*

½   teaspoon unsweetened tropical punch drink mix, *Kool-Aid®*

     Ice cubes

Blue Lagoon

Prep 20 minutes Freeze overnight Makes 4 (8-ounce) servings

Tools you'll need:

* Measuring cups
* 2-quart pitcher
* Wooden spoon
* Ice cube trays
* Needle
* Thread
* Four 6-inch wooden skewers
* 4 large glasses
* 4 drinking straws

Food you'll need:

1   packet (0.22-ounce) unsweetened berry blue or blue raspberry drink mix, *Kool-Aid®*

1   cup sugar

2   quarts water

      Fish-shape candies

4   cups lemonade, *Minute Maid®*

Here's what you do:

1   In a 2-quart pitcher, using a wooden spoon, stir together drink mix, sugar, and water. Pour into ice cube trays. Freeze overnight.

2   Have an adult help you make fishing poles. Using a needle and thread, run a "fishing line" through the heads of 4 fish-shape candies. Tie onto the ends of four 6-inch skewers.

3   To serve, fill 4 large glasses with blue drink mix ice cubes. Add 1 to 2 fish-shape candies and a straw to each glass. Divide chilled lemonade among the glasses. Using a straw, swirl mixture (drink will turn blue as ice cubes melt). Garnish with fishing poles.

Party Idea: Arrange ice cubes in a clean new fish bowl. Pour lemonade over ice cubes; add 4 straws and 8 fish-shape candies. Garnish with fishing poles.

Tropical Cooler

Here's what you do:

1

In a large pitcher, using a large spoon, stir together orange juice, pineapple juice, and apple cider.

2

Place ice cubes in 6 large glasses. Pour orange juice mixture into glasses. Garnish each glass with a pineapple slice and a mint sprig (optional).

Tools you'll need:

* Measuring cups
* Large pitcher
* Large spoon
* 6 large glasses

Food you'll need:

2   cups orange juice,
     Minute Maid®

2   cups pineapple juice, chilled,
     Dole®

2   cups sparkling apple cider,
     chilled, *Martinelli's*®

     Ice cubes

6   canned pineapple slices, *Dole*®
     (optional)

     Fresh mint sprigs (optional)

Mango Tango

Start to Finish 20 minutes Makes 4 (6-ounce) servings

Tools you'll need:

* Measuring cups
* Measuring spoons
* Ice cream scoop
* Medium bowl
* Blender
* Rubber spatula
* 2 glasses
* 2 drinking straws

Food you'll need:

2 cups or more frozen mango chunks, *C&W®*

1½ cups apple juice, *Hansen's®*

1 cup orange sherbet

1 tablespoon instant orange drink powder, *Tang®*

Mango Skewers (optional)

Here's what you do:

1 Place frozen mango chunks in a medium bowl; let stand 10 minutes to thaw slightly.

2 In a blender, place 2 cups of the mango chunks, the apple juice, sherbet, and orange drink powder. Cover; turn on blender. Blend for 1 to 2 minutes or until smooth. Using a rubber spatula, scrape down sides of blender.

3 Pour mixture into 2 glasses. Add a straw to each glass. Garnish with Mango Skewers (optional).

Mango Skewers: Place 2 to 3 mango chunks on each of 2 short skewers.

Minty Chip Frappé

Start to Finish 5 minutes Makes 1 (12-ounce) serving

Here's what you do:

In blender, place ice cream, ice, evaporated milk, chocolate pieces, and chocolate-flavor syrup. Cover; turn blender to high. Blend for about 2 minutes until mixture is smooth and frothy. Using a rubber spatula, scrape down sides of blender. Pour into a large glass. Top with another scoop of ice cream (optional).

Tools you'll need:

* Ice cream scoop
* Measuring cups
* Measuring spoons
* Blender
* Rubber spatula
* 1 large glass

Food you'll need:

2   scoops mint chocolate chip ice cream, *Breyers*®

1   cup crushed ice

$\frac{1}{2}$ cup evaporated milk, *Carnation*®

$\frac{1}{4}$ cup miniature semisweet chocolate pieces, *Nestlé*®

2   tablespoons chocolate-flavor syrup, *Hershey's*®

   Mint chocolate chip ice cream, *Breyers*® (optional)

   Shards of chocolate curls (optional)

Index

Index

About Sandra Lee

Sandra Lee is a *New York Times* best-selling author and a nationally acclaimed lifestyle expert. Her signature Semi-Homemade approach to cooking, home decorating, gardening, crafting, entertaining, beauty, and fashion offers savvy shortcuts and down-to-earth secrets for creating a beautiful, affordable, and most importantly doable lifestyle.

Sandra Lee's cookbook series offers amazing meals in minutes; fabulous food fixin's, and sensational—yet simple—style ideas. *Semi-Homemade Cooking with Sandra Lee* is one of Food Network's hottest cooking shows, providing many helpful hints, timesaving techniques, tips, and tricks.

Find even more creative kid-friendly recipes and ideas online at **semihomemade.com**.

Sandra Lee Semi-Homemade® Cookbook Series
Collect all of these amazingly helpful, timesaving, and beautiful books!
Look for the series wherever quality books are sold.